CHAPTER & VERSE,

CROSSWORDS AND OTHER PUZZLES

~ FUN BIBLE STUDY ~

CHAPTER & VERSE,
CROSSWORDS AND OTHER PUZZLES

~ VERSE VARIETY ~

tjjohnson

authorHOUSE®

AuthorHouseTM
1663 Liberty Drive
Bloomington, IN 47403
www.authorhouse.com
Phone: 1-800-839-8640

First published by AuthorHouse 09/30/2011

ISBN: 978-1-4670-4208-6 (sc)
ISBN: 978-1-4670-4207-9 (ebk)

Printed in the United States of America
Bloomington, Indiana

This book is printed on acid-free paper.

DEDICATION

This book is dedicated to:

Those who are genuinely looking to

Increase their knowledge of God's Word

And to align their thoughts and ways accordingly;

So as to please God,

So as to help someone else,

So that our lives may be enriched

As we pass through this age

On Earth.

I wish you God's Continued Favor,

and His Everlasting Peace!

HELPFUL HINTS

Although all Bible References are from

The King James Study Bible

Any Bible will do to help with translation

Helpful also is a concordance, a Bible Dictionary

And/Or use of a computer for access to

Web-based Bible searches.

To find correct squares for crossword puzzle entries,

read the puzzle numbers from left to right,

Horizontally, line by line,

whether the clue is Across or Down

(Ch) is used to indicate Chapter

(V) is used to indicate Verse of puzzle reference Chapter

~ Acknowledgements ~

To:

My Christian brothers and sisters
of Bayview Baptist Church in San Diego, California
Where I discovered that God has given all of us
A Special Gift, and
Where I am learning to use and appreciate mine.

So many people encouraged me
With valuable remarks and suggestions
Feeding my soul with that food we all need:
Encouragement, validation, confirmation.

Carolyn Denese Wright has an exceptional gift of exhortation,
Knowing intuitively when a person needs reassurance,
And always offers kind and heartening words
To help me remain motivated and productive.

Carrie Lillie Alexander, a long-time friend,
Stoked my writer's senses early on
By planting deep inside my psyche
A Seed, A Hope, A Dream,
To one day recognize the talent
That God had given me.

Special Thanks To:
Shelvy Barmer, who power proofed my work;
Ruthie Wilson, who supplied occasional photography;
Sharon Cawthorne, who contributed insightful marketing ideas;
Bill Harris and Reverend Peter Zindler for their valuable critiques.

TABLE OF CONTENTS

~ PUZZLE CONTENTS CONTINUED~

~ PUZZLE CONTENTS CONTINUED~

~ APPENDIX A ~

PUZZLE ANSWERS

~ APPENDIX A ~
ANSWERS CONTINUED

~ APPENDIX A ~
ANSWERS CONTINUED

INTRODUCTION

This book of puzzles is designed as an aid for studying various Bible chapters and/or verses. Not concentrating on any particular chapter, it rather focuses on a variety of chapters and verses. It can be an excellent tool to help maintain information that you have previously read, while at the same time, exercising your brain and feeding your soul. Bible study can be very interesting and lots of fun.

Each puzzle is based on information taken from *The King James Study Bible.* In reading and solving the puzzles, you will encounter words and phrases you think you understand. However, it is advisable to use a good Bible Dictionary and concordance for Old Testament (Hebrew) and New Testament (Greek) translations even for common words. Because, words we use everyday often have a completely different connotation in presentation of Biblical stories and situations. Word usage and translation depend heavily on how the word is used in each occurrence. There is plenty of Bible based information on the Internet; and you'll find one that you like best by trial and error. Many Bibles also give translations for certain words.

Again, puzzles in this book review selected Bible chapters and verses. I hope you enjoy solving these puzzles as much as I have enjoyed writing them. And I pray they accomplish that which they're designed to do—help you study and learn the Bible.

May God continue to make His Face shine upon you,

tjjohnson

Now,
Write it before them
In a table,
And note it in a
Book
That it may be for
Time . . .
To come . . .
For ever, And . . .
Ever.

From Isaiah 30:8

Acts of the Apostles, No. 1
Acts 1-9, KJV

(Note: Numbers read from left to right, line by line, whether clue is Across or Down)

Acts of the Apostles, No. 1
Across Clues:

4. _____ replaced Judas as an apostle; 1:25-26.
6. Jesus was called the _____ One in Acts 8:52.
7. Peter and John were sprung from jail by an _____,
9. The Jews tried to _____ Saul also.
11. Before he was Paul, he was _____.
12. Barnabas is interpreted as the _____ of consolation or encouragement; 4:36.
14. After his experience with the extraordinary light, Saul could not see for _____ days.
16. _____ preached on the Day of Pentecost.
17. Philip baptized an Ethiopian _____ as he traveled to Gaza; 8:27.
18. God used a disciple of Damascus named _____ to help Saul after his ordeal; 9:10-11.
19. Paul was formerly a _____ in persecuting the church at Jerusalem.
21. When Stephen died, he was calling upon ____.
23. The Jewish council forbade Peter and John to speak the name, _____.
25. Stephen told the _____ that he saw the Son of man standing on the right hand of God; 7:51-56.
28. On the day of Pentecost, ____ thousand were baptized; 2:41.
29. He was stoned to death.
33. Tabitha and _____ are the same; 9:36.
36. The early believers worshipped together in someone's _____.
37. He is credited for writing the book of Acts.
41. Bethsaida translates to 'house of ____.'
42. The apostles had all things in _____.
43. The lame man that Peter commanded to walk was over _____ years old; 4:22.
45. Simon the sorcerer believed in Jesus Christ, and was baptized, but he tried to ____ the power to invoke the Holy Ghost; 8:9-13, 18-19.
46. The Lord referred to Saul as a chosen _____; 9:15.
48. God healed a man through Peter who had been bed ridden for _____ years; 9:32-35.
50. Peter, _____, John: the privileged inner circle.
51. Paul was of the tribe of _____. (Phil 3:5).
53. A voice from the bright light asked Saul, 'why do you persecute ____?'
55. The Holy Spirit fell like tongues of ____; 2:3.
56. Today, _____ is a major city named Jaffa, & part of Tel Aviv-Jaffa municipality.
57. Gamaliel warned the council that if the disciples work was not of God, then they would amount to _____; 5:39.
58. Before the gospel was taken to the Gentiles, it was preached to the Jews _____ ; 2:39, 3:26, Rom 1:16, 2;10.
59. Even though the apostles were beaten and thrown in jail, they did not _____ to teach/preach the name of Jesus.
60. The_____ of salvation is through Jesus Christ only; 3:26.

(Down Clues Next Page)

Acts of the Apostles, No. 1
Down Clues:

1. Peter accused the Jews of killing _____.
2. Paul learned at the feet of _____; 5:34.
3. Tabitha was a woman of good works and charitable _____; 9:36.
5. Philip preached to the people of _____;   8:5.
8. Stephen did great _____ among the people; 6:8.
10. Gamaliel was a teacher of the _____.
13. Peter, Andrew, James, & John, & Philip were from the town of _____; Matt 4:18.
15. Saul was on his way to Damascus when he met _____.
20. Peter told the lame man to '____ up and walk ; 2:6.
22. Acts 2:30 refers to _____ as a prophet.
24. The men who were with Saul on the Damascus road heard a voice, but they didn't _____ anyone.
25. Peter and _____ met a lame man at the temple gate.
26. _____ disciples were chosen to administer to the needs of widows and others; 6:1-3.
27. Saul was of the city of _____ ; 9:11.
30. Saul received the _____ Ghost and was baptized, and began to preach the gospel shortly thereafter; 9:18-20.
31. The Jewish leaders were not pleased with the disciples preaching in the ____ of Jesus.
32. The high priest, other priests, elders, & leaders of the community comprised the _____.
34. Stephen saw the _____ of God; 7:55.
35. After Stephen's death, some laid their clothes at the _____ of Saul.
38. Pentecost translates to _____.
39. _____ proclaimed Saul's authenticity; 9:26-27.
40. This puzzle created by tj _____, (4.20.05).
44. Saul tried to join forces with the disciples at Jerusalem, but they didn't _____ that he was one of them.
46. Saul had a _____ that a certain man of Damascus would help him; 9:12.
47. Peter pleaded with the Jews to _____ ; 2:38.
49. Paul was chosen by God to take His Word to the _____; 9:15.
52. Cornelius was a _____ centurion in Caesarea; 10:1.
53. In Acts 8, Simon was a man of sorcery or _____.
54. Peter said to Tabitha, "_____," and she got up from her death bed; 9:37, 40.

Acts of the Apostles, No. 2; Acts 10, KJV
(Puzzle Grid found on Page 7)

Clues Across:

3. The Roman centurion lived in this city.
6. An angel spoke to Cornelius in a _____.
9. _____ relates to ethnos or ethnic difference.
10. This puzzled created by tj _____, (04.20.05).
14. These are they whom Jesus chose to spread His Word.
15. God used a _____ man, a tanner, and a dream to help Peter change his mind about unclean things.
16. John the Baptist preached about the _____ of Jesus Christ.
18. Fear in relation to God translates to reverence or _____.
21. God raised Jesus up on the _____ day.
23. A centurion was a _____ military officer.
24. _____ told Peter about his vision.
25. Cornelius _____ down to worship Peter.
28. A band or cohort is comprised of about _____ hundred men.
29. Peter went up to the housetop about the _____ hour to pray.
30. A vision can be said to be a deep trance or _____.
32. Cornelius _____ God.
38. _____ is known as the apostle to bring the Word to the Gentiles.
40. It was _____ for a Jew to keep company with one that was not a Jew.
42. The Jews were astonished because the _____ also received the Holy Ghost.
43. This term refers to dialects which define languages and is different among nations.
48. Anyone who reveres God and is righteous is _____ by Him.
49. Peter heard a _____ that told him to eat the things he saw in his vision.
51. The apostle, Simon _____.
52. The apostles ate and drank with _____ after He was raised from death.
53. Verse 43 reads _____, not sin.
54. The next _____ Peter went with the men that Cornelius had sent.
55. Peter was a guest in Joppa at the house of a man named _____.
57. The Holy Spirit is a _____ from God.
59. Three men were dispatched to go in _____ of Peter.
62. _____ before, Peter denied the Lord three times.
63. Peter translates as the Greek word <u>petros</u> which means a _____ or stone.
64. Cornelius was a _____ man.
65. 'Not so, _____,' said Peter.
66. _____ means the same as three.

(Down Clues Next Page)

Chapter & Verse

Acts of the Apostles, No. 2
Acts 10, KJV

Clues Down:

1. The housetop is the same as a rooftop _____.
2. Peter advised Cornelius that he himself was just a _____, not one to bow down to.
4. Peter's host was a _____ by trade.
5. Everyone who heard Peter speak was also _____ in the name of the Lord.
7. Cornelius was of the _____ band or regiment.
8. What God has cleaned is not considered _____.
10. The apostle Peter was given this surname by _____.
11. Cornelius was a centurion or _____.
12. God's _____ was published throughout all Judea.
13. Cornelius had invited his relatives and _____ to hear Peter speak.
17. Peter fell into a _____ thinking about food.
19. The ninth hour equates to _____ o'clock pm.
20. There were all manner of _____ in Peter's vision.
22. The Jews are charged to have slain Jesus and _____ Him on a tree.
26. _____ is credited with writing Acts.
27. Whosoever believes in Jesus _____ receive a pardon for their sins.
31. Peter _____ the invitation to kill and eat the beasts in his vision.
33. The Holy Spirit fell on _____ that heard the Word.
34. Peter is known as the apostle who brought God's Word to the _____.
35. The Spirit told Peter to _____ nothing.
36. Jesus was ordained by God to be the Judge of the _____ and the dead.
37. The _____ Testament is full of prophecy that is fulfilled in the New Testament.
39. God _____ Jesus with the Holy Ghost.
41. The vessel in Peter's vision looked like a _____.
44. The Holy _____ fell on all who heard Peter speak that day.
45. God showed Peter that he should not call any man common or _____.
46. The Holy Spirit & the Holy Ghost are the _____.
47. God is no respecter of _____.
49. Peter had a vision of a _____ descending from heaven.
50. Cornelius had a vision about the _____ hour of the day.
51. All in the house began to _____ God.
55. The _____ told Peter how many men were at the door of Simon the tanner's house.
56. Peter declared that he had never _____ anything that was unclean.
58. The voice of the vision spoke to Peter three _____.
60. Cornelius had a _____ reputation among the Jews.
61. This hour translates to the sixth hour.

Acts of the Apostles, No. 2, Acts 10, KJV

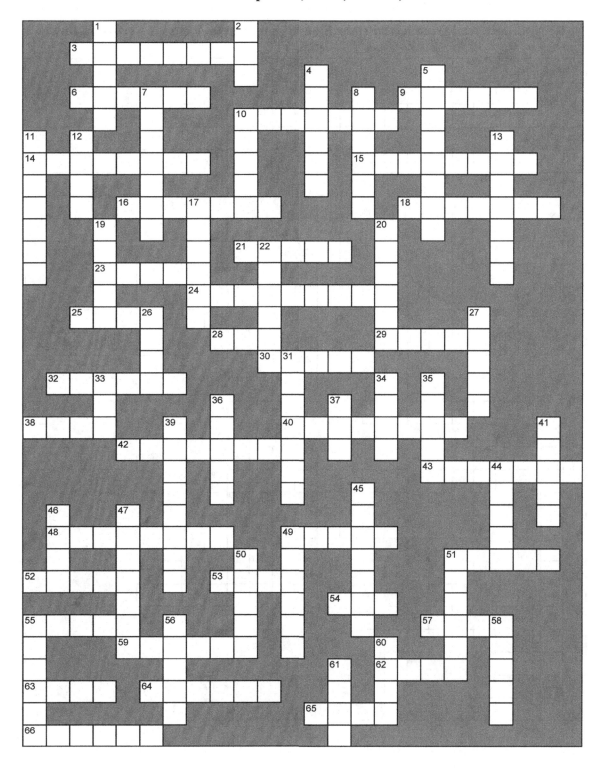

A Covenant Study, Various Scripture, KJV

(Note: Numbers read from left to right, line by line, whether clue is Across or Down.

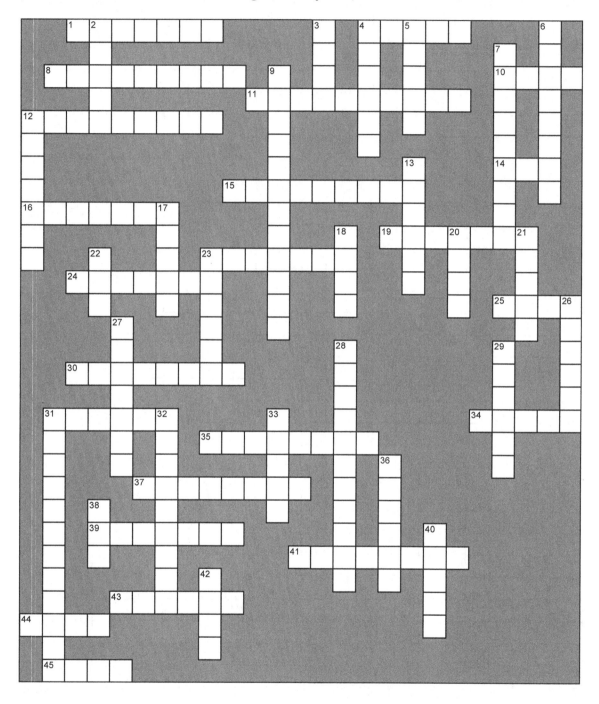

Covenant Clues:
Across:

1. King David's son _____ did not keep the covenant that God made with his ancestors, (1Ki 11:11).
4. First usage of covenant in the _____ is at Genesis 6:18.
8. The new covenant is a promise based upon a _____ awakening; (Heb 8:6) (see 11A).
10. Job said in chapter 31:1 that he made a covenant with his _____.
11. The old covenant differs from the new covenant in that it was based upon _____ to be kept; (Ex 19:5; Heb 8:9) (see 8A).
12. Merriam-Webster defines a covenant as an _____, or a pact, or a will, or a promise, or a testament.[1,2]
14. An example of a covenant between two ____ is given in Genesis 21:27, and 31:43-44.
15. Paul declared himself and other apostles to be _____ of the new covenant, (2 Cor. 3:6).
16. The LORD proclaimed he was an _____ to Israel, (Jer. 31:32; Hosea 2:19-20).
19. A covenant of the _____ is described in Exodus 31:12-18.
23. The LORD accused the _____ of corrupting the covenant of Levi, (Mal 2:4-9).
24. (From 23A) '. . . because they profaned the covenant by being _____ in the law causing many people to stumble,' (Mal 2:1-9).
25. Only the tribe of ____ was permitted to carry the ark of the covenant.
30. The land God allocated to Abram and his seed was described as the _____ land, (Ex 12:25; Deut 6:3).
31. The new covenant was not established until _____, (Matt 26:28; 1 Cor. 11:25; Lu 22:7-23; Rom 11:27).
34. In Genesis 9:11, God promised never to destroy the world again by a _____.
35. Genesis 17:2 presents an additional covenant between God and Abraham to _____ his seed.
37. The Old Testament (OT) is said to be the old _____.
39. The sign of the covenant between God and Noah was the _____, Gen 9:12-17).
41. Close friends, David and _____, made a covenant between themselves, (1 Sam 18:3).
43. God's promise to Abram involved land that originally belonged to Noah's grandson _____, (Gen 9:18, 25, 26).
44. (See 13 D) . . . For this [is] my covenant unto them, when I shall take away their _____, (Rom 11:27).
45. The covenant in Genesis six is between God and _____.

(Down Clues Next Page)

9

Covenant Clues Continued:
Down:

2. In Leviticus, the covenant involves _____ oil.
3. The covenant in Genesis 15:18 involves a _____ grant.
4. Jesus is mediator of the new covenant which is superior or _____ than the old, (Heb 8:6, 12:24).
5. The _____ of the covenant refers to the blood Christ gave to forgive our sins, (Heb 10:29, 13:20).
6. Punishment for _____ God's covenant is described in Leviticus 26:14-46.
7. The new covenant is translated as the new _____, (2Cor 3:6; Heb 8:8) [3,4]
9. The covenant that took 40 days and 40 nights to complete was that of the ten _____, (Ex 34:28).
12. Abram was renamed _____, in Genesis 17:5.
13. All _____ shall be saved as it is written, for the Deliverer shall turn away ungodliness from Jacob, (to 44A), (Rom 11:26).
17. Jonathan made a covenant with the house of _____ that kindness be continued to his descendants, (1Sam20:14-16).
18. The covenant with Edom was a brotherly covenant because of _____, (Amos 1:6).
20. Exodus 24:4-7 speaks of a _____ of the covenant.
21. A gift of land flowing with milk and _____ was part of covenant with forefathers of Israel, (Jer11:6).
22. Joash, king of Judah, renewed the covenant with the LORD after the book of ___ was found by Hilkiah in 2Ki22:8.
23. Between God and man, a covenant is better defined as a _____ or promise. [5]
26. God's prophecy for his new covenant; "I will put my law in their _____ parts, and write it in their hearts, Jer. 31:33.
27. In marriage, a covenant is a _____.
28. The LORD's covenant with Abraham was to be _____.
29. What Moses brought down from Mount Horeb is referred to as the _____ or tablets of the covenant, (Deu. 9:9).
31. The covenant in Genesis 17:10 between God, Abraham, and his seed was that of the _____.
32. _____ designed this puzzle June 24th, 2008.
33. The covenant that God set forth in the Old Testament was written on _____ tablets, (2Cor 3:3).
36. The first covenant had _____, prompting the need for a new covenant, (Heb 8:7).
38. Numbers 10:33 established the _____ of the covenant.
40. When people _____, they make a covenant with each other.
42. Making a covenant usually involves the swearing of an ____.

[1] www.Merriam-Webster.com
[2,4] Merrill F. Unger, *Unger's Bible Dictionary,* 3rd Ed. (1957; reprint, Chicago: Moody Press, 1981), 224.
[3,5] www.blueletterbible.org

Entering Into A Covenant

There are many other covenants written of in the Bible. The preceding puzzle addressed just a few of them.

The first covenant found in the Bible is in Genesis 6:18. This verse speaks of the covenant that God made with Noah in preparing the ark, which saved Noah, his family, and every animal species there was, male and female, from the flood that destroyed the world of those days.

Genesis 6:14-22:

14) "Make thee an ark of gopher wood; rooms shalt thou make in the ark, and shalt pitch it within and without with pitch.

15) And this [is the fashion] which thou shalt make it [of]: The length of the ark [shall be] three hundred cubits, the breadth of it fifty cubits, and the height of it thirty cubits.

16) A window shalt thou make to the ark, and in a cubit shalt thou finish it above; and the door of the ark shalt thou set in the side thereof; [with] lower, second, and third [stories] shalt thou make it.

17) And, behold, I, even I, do bring a flood of waters upon the earth, to destroy all flesh, wherein [is] the breath of life, from under heaven; [and] every thing that [is] in the earth shall die.

18) But with thee will I establish my covenant; and thou shalt come into the ark, thou, and thy sons, and thy wife, and thy sons' wives with thee.

19) And of every living thing of all flesh, two of every [sort] shalt thou bring into the ark, to keep [them] alive with thee; they shall be male and female.

20) Of fowls after their kind, and of cattle after their kind, of every creeping thing of the earth after his kind, two of every [sort] shall come unto thee, to keep [them] alive.

21) And take thou unto thee of all food that is eaten, and thou shalt gather [it] to thee; and it shall be for food for thee, and for them.

22) Thus did Noah; according to all that God commanded him, so did he."

A Letter of Concern, No. 1
1 Thessalonians 1 & 2, KJV

(Note: Numbers read from left to right, line by line, whether clue is Across or Down; & number of spaces does not necessarily indicate letters in an answer.)

Across:

2. Paul preached the gospel with much _ _ _ _ _.
4. (One of the attributes of 1 Thessalonians 1:3) _ _ _ _ _ _ _ _ of hope in our Lord Jesus Christ.
9. Paul remembered the brethren's work of _ _ _ _ _ and love.
11. English word for epistle.
13. Paul and his companions' work is referred to as a _ _ _ _ _ of love.
14. This is how the early gospel converts were treated by Paul.
15. Paul's followers were examples to neighboring Macedonia and _ _ _ _ _ _.
17. A familiar word used in the salutation of Paul's epistle was _ _ _ _ _ _ _.

Letter of Concern No. 1
Across Clues Continued:

19. Paul declared that they did not seek _ _ _ _ _ for the work being done.
21. An affectionate term for the brethren.
22. Paul bragged about how they had turned away from _ _ _ _ _ to serve the living true God.
23. This puzzle content created by _ _ _ _ _ _ _ (11.14.2004).
25. One of Paul's traveling companions during this time was _ _ _ _ _ _.
27. These early Christians did not care about pleasing _ _ _.
28. The Hebrew word for Silvanus.
29. Paul reported how he had been _ _ _ _ _ _ _ _ _ treated in Philippi
32. He reminded the church that they were _ _ _ _ _ _ _ by God.
33. Paul was _ _ _ _ in his worship and proclamation of God.
34. What hindered a personal visit from the missionaries and Paul?
35. Another word for exhort.
36. In Bible days, this land was known as the land of the Jews.
37. The work of Paul and the early church were _ _ _ _ _ and tested daily.

Down:

1. These people is said to have killed their own prophets, one of them the Lord Jesus.
3. The young church was advised to _ _ _ _ for the Son from heaven.
4. Who was author of the book of Thessalonians?
5. The believers at Thessalonica endured much _ _ _ _ _ _ _ _ _ _, just as Paul had.
6. Paul's emissaries did not want to be a _ _ _ _ _ _ to anyone.
7. God's word works effectively in those who _ _ _ _ _ _ _.
8. Paul _ _ _ _ _ _ _ to visit Thessalonica himself.
10. To _ _ _ _ upright refers to the Christian way of life.
12. Chapter 2, verse 3 says that the gospel was not brought in _ _ _ _ _ nor in error.
16. Complete this phrase: The Lord Jesus _ _ _ _ _ _.
18. The Greek translation of the word church is _ _ _ _ _ _ _ _.
19. Some of the early church did not want the gospel spread among the _ _ _ _ _ _ _ _.
20. Paul's exhortation to the church was also backed by the Holy _ _ _ _ _.
24. Paul heard that the church at Thessalonica was confused about the _ _ _ _ _ _ coming of Christ.
26. To follow someone's lead is to _ _ _ _ _ _ _ their actions.
30. Peace from God our _ _ _ _ _.
31. Word of the gospel was heard not only in the local cities, but was spread _ _ _ _ _ _.
36. This epistle declared the church at Thessalonica as having glory and _ _ _.

Chapter & Verse

A Letter of Concern, No. 2
1 Thessalonians 3, 4, 5; KJV

(Note: Numbers read from left to right, whether clue is Across or Down, & number of spaces does not necessarily indicate letters in an answer.)

Across:
3. The day of the Lord will come as a _ _ _ _ _ in the night.
5. This letter encourages living a _ _ _ _ _ life.
6. Paul was happy to hear the good _ _ _ _ _ _ _ concerning the Thessalonians.
10. The chief of angels is the _ _ _ _ _ _ _ _ _.
12. _ _ _ _ _hearted people are said to be feebleminded.
15. Those who don't believe in the Lord Jesus Christ live in _ _ _ _ _ _ _.

14

16. Christians who are still alive when Jesus returns will be _ _ _ _ _ _ up with Him.
18. Paul's emissary was a _ _ _ _ _ _ laborer in the gospel.
19. When Christ returns, he will descend from heaven with a shout and the _ _ _ _ of God.
20. Christians live in the _ _ _ _ of salvation.
21. To comfort is to _ _ _ _ _ _ _ _.
23. Those who are not of the Lord will suffer pain as a woman in _ _ _ _ _.
25. The church is encouraged to _ _ _ _ those who provide instruction in the Lord.
27. Paul urged the Thessalonian converts to walk in such a way as to _ _ _ _ _ God.
28. Paul describes the dead as being _ _ _ _ _.
29. It is written that we should not quench the _ _ _ _ _ _.
31. Paul taught to _ _ _ _ without ceasing.
32. Greet all the brethren with a _ _ _ _ kiss.
34. We must not fret for the Lord is the _ _ _ _ _ _ _ of all wrong-doing.
35. Those who are insubordinate are said to be _ _ _ _ _ _.
37. _ _ _ _ _ _ _ created the content of this puzzle, (11.15.2004).
40. Christians are said to be children of the _ _ _ _ _, and of the day.
42. Whether we are _ _ _ _ or asleep, Christians shall live together with Christ forever.
43. A grand meeting will take place in the _ _ _ _ _ _ when the rapture takes place.
44. We are reminded to not be in _ _ _ _ _ _ for those who have died.

Down:

1. To cheat is to _ _ _ _ _ _ _.
2. _ _ _ _ is a passion the church is warned to overcome.
4. To stand fast in the Lord is to _ _ _ _ according to His Word.
7. 'I would not have you _ _ _ _ _ _ _ _, brethren.'
8. The church was reminded that they would _ _ _ _ _ _ tribulations.
9. Paul longed to see the _ _ _ _ _ of the brethren he had taught Jesus to.
11. Paul considered himself the _ _ _ _ _ among the apostles.
13. Christians must abstain from any form or appearance of _ _ _ _.
14. To exalt is to _ _ _ _ _ _ _ (2 words).
15. If you reject God's word, you _ _ _ _ _ _ _ God.
17. Another term for sexual immorality is _ _ _ _ _ _ _ _ _ _.
18. Believers are warned to arm ourselves with _ _ _ _ _ and love.
19. In everything we must give _ _ _ _ _ _.
20. God has called us unto _ _ _ _ _ _ _ _
22. Paul addresses his followers at Thessalonica as _ _ _ _ _ _ _ _.
24. He was sent to encourage and strengthen the church at Thessalonica.
26. Jesus died so that we may have _ _ _ _ _ _ _ _ _.
30. Christians who have died will rise _ _ _ _ _.
33. They prayed night and day to complete the teaching of those _ _ _ _ _ in the faith.
34. The church is urged to _ _ _ _ _ doing evil for evil.
36. The news of faith and _ _ _ _ pleased Paul and his brethren.
38. Paul spoke of his authority as given to him by the Lord _ _ _ _ _.
39. Fearing his preaching might be in _ _ _ _ _, Paul exhorted the church fervently.
41. No one knows the exact _ _ _ _ or day of the Lord's return.

Chapter & Verse

Books of the New Testament

Find the New Testament Books in the grid and circle. Words can go across, down and in two diagonals. Some words share a letter. You may also find unscripted words in the puzzle grid.

```
2  T  H  E  S  S  A  L  O  N  I  A  N  S  W  B  Z  B  T  L  L
1  K  R  T  B  L  X  2  P  E  T  E  R  W  Z  X  Y  K  N  T  K
L  C  D  E  H  P  Q  M  E  P  H  E  S  I  A  N  S  D  N  T  C
R  B  O  T  V  1  T  H  E  S  S  A  L  O  N  I  A  N  S  Y  O
C  J  C  R  G  E  M  A  R  K  S  K  Y  Z  W  T  K  N  H  J  L
P  N  W  N  I  K  L  N  K  N  C  H  C  E  X  L  W  T  R  A  O
Z  X  R  B  S  N  R  A  A  1  T  M  H  L  R  G  U  K  T  M  S
Q  M  X  T  V  E  T  I  T  O  J  T  V  G  R  N  T  K  N  E  S
C  T  C  T  T  F  T  H  M  I  T  O  M  T  M  W  M  C  E  S  I
V  A  G  E  D  A  R  I  I  A  O  V  H  N  T  X  R  M  M  2  A
G  H  P  P  L  X  T  K  M  A  C  N  O  N  I  X  C  M  N  C  N
2  1  E  A  H  1  G  H  L  G  N  M  L  M  T  L  R  C  L  O  S
T  T  G  B  H  I  K  T  K  W  E  S  M  M  U  P  H  V  N  R  R
J  K  I  M  R  H  L  B  K  L  V  F  W  G  S  Q  X  N  L  I  L
J  T  W  M  N  E  M  I  I  N  L  R  O  M  A  N  S  T  Q  N  T
O  J  R  F  O  G  W  H  P  L  D  R  N  N  T  M  N  V  B  T  T
H  K  W  D  F  T  P  S  X  P  Y  J  M  T  P  K  N  2  T  H  H
N  L  J  P  D  N  H  T  R  L  I  N  C  Z  X  H  L  J  N  I  M
S  Y  O  R  R  P  P  Y  M  R  K  A  W  X  O  M  D  O  K  A  Z
O  F  H  K  B  T  X  C  P  L  K  C  N  J  T  K  N  H  V  N  F
N  K  N  C  J  U  D  E  J  F  B  B  3  S  V  Y  V  N  D  S  T
```

Clues for New Testament Books,
Circle in the puzzle grid on previous page.

1 Corinthians	1 John	1 Peter
1 Thessalonians	1 Timothy	2 Corinthians
2 John	2 Peter	2 Thessalonians
2 Timothy	3 John	Acts
Colossians	Ephesians	Galatians
Hebrews	James	John
Jude	Luke	Mark
Matthew	Philemon	Philippians
Revelation		
Romans		
Titus		

tjjohnson, (Puzzle creator, 11.05.2010)

Books of the Old Testament

Find the Old Testament Books of the Bible in the grid and circle. Words may share letters, can go across, down and in two diagonals. You may also find unscripted words in the puzzle grid.

```
R  V  2  C  H  R  O  N  I  C  L  E  S  Z  E  C  H  A  R  I  A  H  W
C  N  P  V  R  Y  D  J  V  I  K  L  D  B  A  M  O  S  Y  Y  2  X  E
R  N  A  H  U  M  R  L  A  G  X  2  S  A  M  U  E  L  N  R  K  Z  C
W  J  C  Y  L  X  E  G  C  H  L  K  R  D  N  F  M  G  C  K  I  Q  C
T  K  N  K  M  U  G  M  L  H  T  F  U  X  M  I  Y  Z  C  M  N  L  L
L  H  B  B  M  A  R  Z  A  E  S  L  T  C  N  X  E  H  P  L  G  N  E
F  W  M  A  H  R  E  C  K  I  V  S  H  O  D  P  Y  L  R  Z  S  M  S
H  Y  S  B  R  X  I  Z  S  V  N  I  M  V  F  T  M  Y  O  J  Z  B  I
B  1  C  C  G  M  R  E  R  O  T  O  T  P  R  S  M  Y  V  O  E  C  A
X  N  K  T  L  E  N  N  I  A  L  B  Y  I  E  Z  L  L  E  N  P  V  S
Z  H  N  M  H  E  K  T  B  O  K  M  G  L  C  N  F  Z  R  A  H  F  T
L  O  G  T  G  R  A  N  S  V  O  R  C  V  L  U  Q  T  B  H  A  K  E
J  S  S  K  Q  T  P  F  Z  N  M  I  M  Y  P  P  S  H  S  N  N  N  S
K  E  H  O  N  W  O  S  O  L  N  Y  E  X  O  D  U  S  J  E  I  U  Q
W  A  R  E  B  G  D  R  A  O  J  O  S  H  U  A  N  T  L  H  A  M  T
T  C  M  E  N  A  E  H  R  L  X  L  J  Q  C  R  G  E  N  E  H  B  J
M  A  L  O  M  T  D  H  A  K  M  T  T  U  C  M  O  B  M  M  M  E  J
L  C  S  M  U  I  C  I  1  B  G  S  K  L  D  J  A  L  R  I  F  R  O
K  N  M  E  L  1  A  T  A  K  A  Z  J  O  B  G  M  L  V  A  X  S  H
Z  B  D  N  K  L  V  H  G  H  I  K  F  L  F  Z  E  R  A  H  Z  C  N
K  B  E  Z  E  K  I  E  L  T  C  N  K  X  W  P  R  S  D  C  R  T  S
V  R  I  S  A  I  A  H  Z  C  P  Y  G  U  D  B  F  Y  L  C  H  T  O
W  G  X  L  K  C  Q  X  L  L  R  L  N  S  K  D  V  V  G  X  Q  I  N
```

Clues for Old Testament Books
Circle words in the puzzle grid on previous page.

1 Chronicles	2 Chronicles	1 Kings
2 Kings	1 Samuel	2 Samuel
Amos	Daniel	Deuteronomy
Ecclesiastes	Esther	Exodus
Ezekiel	Ezra	Genesis
Habakkuk	Haggai	Hosea
Isaiah	Jeremiah	Job
Joel	Jonah	Joshua
Judges	Lamentations	Leviticus
Malachi	Micah	Nahum
Nehemiah	Numbers	Obadiah
Proverbs	Psalms	Ruth

Song of Solomon
Zechariah
Zephaniah

TJJohnson, (Puzzle creator, 11.05.2010)

Faith And Temptation
Jude, KJV

(Numbers read from left to right, line by line regardless of Across or Down clues)

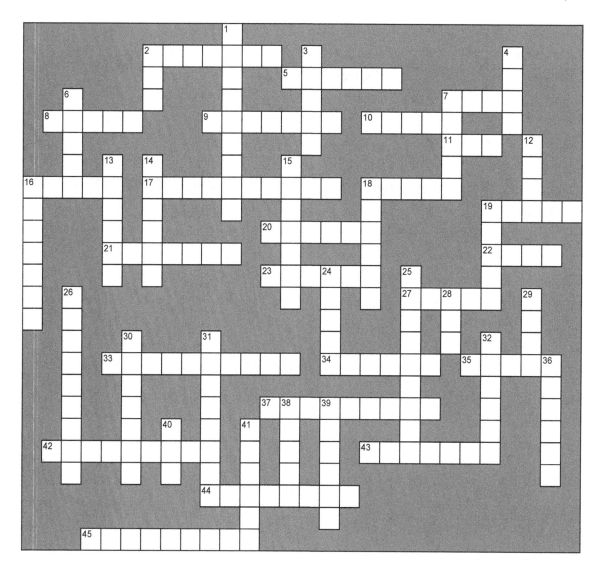

Across:

2. An identification of Jude is that as _____ of Jesus Christ.

5. Korah/Core wanted to invade the office of an Israelite _____, (Numbers 16:3).

7. Cain murdered his brother _____.

8. The only way to know the _____ is to study God's Word, and pray for understanding.

9. Words in _____ have been added for clarification to Bible scriptures.

10. Korah challenged the authority of Moses and _____.

11. Jude calls _____ wise, glorious, majestic, and powerful forever.

16. Clouds without_____.

17. Vengeance in verse seven translates as _____.

Faith & Temptation Across Continued:

18. The _____ is said to be the 'prince of the world', (John 12:31; 14:30; 16:11; Eph 2:2).
19. Jude is sometimes spelled as _____ or Judah in the New Testament.
20. First estate in v6 refers to their proper _____ or place.
21. This book of Jude is a/an _____.
22. Christians should _____ those close to being led astray.
23. Save in verse 23 means to _____.
27. False teachers deny _____.
33. Beloved is a term of _____.
34. Verse eight speaks of despicable people as _____ dreamers.
35. Jude declares himself as the brother of _____.
37. The _____ of darkness is reserved for those whom Jude warned Christians about.
42. Gainsaying in verse 11 refers to _____.
43. _____ in verse three means to struggle or fight for.
44. False teachers cause _____ among those who are unsure of their belief.
45. A mocker scoffs, jeers, or _____.

Down:

1. Jesus will present us _____ before God.
2. Raging waves of the _____.
3. We are to be aware of those who turn the _____ of God into lasciviousness.
4. Jude is the _____ epistle of the Bible to have one chapter.
6. Trees with no _____.
7. Satan was originally a/an _____.
12. To be lascivious is to be _____.
13. Christians are advised to keep themselves built up by _____.
14. Verse 19 says they do not have the _____.
15. The readers are addressed as _____.
16. Sensual in verse 19 translates as _____.
18. The Lord made Balaam's _____ talk.
19. Both Jude and James are half-brothers of _____.
24. Michael is the _____ angel.
25. This puzzle created by _____, (04.20.2005).
26. Michael is also the _____.
28. Balaam caused Israel to _____.
29. Sodom and Gomorrah were destroyed by _____.
30. Jude calls false teachers _____.
31. Jude writes that false teachers/preachers were _____ to be condemned.
32. _____ in verse one means to be invited or selected.
36. Fornication refers to _____ immorality.
38. These mockers follow their own _____.
39. Salvation, in verse three, is described as both _____ and most valuable.
40. 'Now to _____ who is able to keep us from falling . . .'
41. Those who mislead others by distorting God's word are often referred to as sheep in _____ clothing.

Gird Up Your Loins
1 Peter 1:13-25, KJV

Across Clues:

1. Silver and gold are considered as _____ things.
5. God judges us according to every man's/woman's _____.
7. Gird can mean to _____.
9. Prepare for action.
10. Aimless conversation is considered to be_____.
11. To be _____ is decided before the foundation of the world.
12. 'Be ye holy, for I am _____.'
14. To be calm, collected.
15. The son.
17. To be evil is to be _____.
20. Christ is also called, 'The ____ of God.'
24. Things that are _____ can be silver, gold, houses, cars, stuff.
27. To respect God is to be in _____ of him.
29. One's loins describe the _____.
32. The Christians in this chapter were to defend their _____.
35. The Word of the Lord _____ forever.
36. This Bible book written by _____.
37. The writer asks us to remain _____ in the revelation of Jesus Christ.
40. We were created by God, but are to be _____ again.
41. He who created us is described as being _____.
42. All flesh is like the _____.
43. Followers of Christ are to be _____ as children.
44. Believers are in _____ of, and respect the power of God.

Down:

1. Our God is not _____ to one above another.
2. The body of Jesus represented a lamb without _____.
3. Peter refers to the blood of Christ as being _____.
4. 'All the ____ of man is like the flower of grass.'
6. Fear in verse 17 alludes to _____.
8. _____ is a Spirit, (John 4:24; 1Peter 3:4).
13. In our former _____ we were ignorant of God's Word.
16. Peter advised the church to hope to the end for ____.
18. God judges without _____ of one person over another.
19. God's Word _____ and abides forever.
21. Conversation refers to our way we live our life, our _____.
22. An epistle is a _____.
23. This puzzle created by tj _____ on 11.29.07.
25. Christ redeemed us with His _____.
26. Peter advised the early church to prepare their _____.
28. The _____ of God is incorruptible.
30. Determine beforehand.

Gird Up Your Loins, Down Clues Continued:

31. Love one another with a _____ heart.
33. To 'gird up our minds' is to be _____ and attentive to the matter at hand.
34. The Comforter, (2 words), (John 14:26, hint: alternate name).
38. The Father.
39. God is _____.

Gird Up Your Loins
1 Peter 1:13-25, KJV

(Note: Puzzle numbers read from left to right regardless of Across or Down clues)

Go For What You Know
Various, KJV

(Note: Numbers read left to right, whether clue is Across or Down)

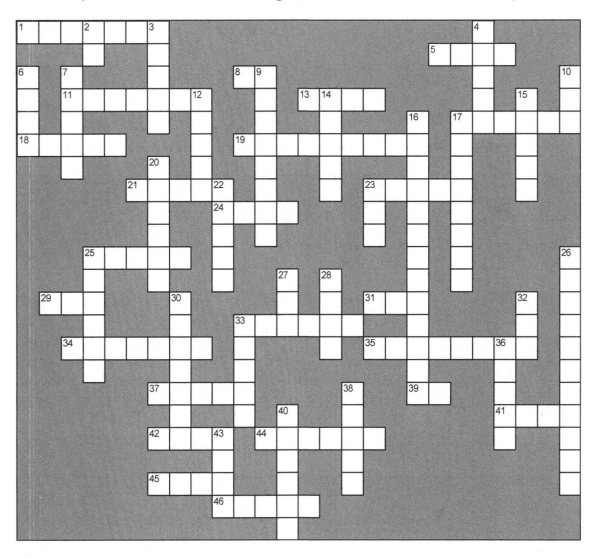

Across:

1. Abraham's first son.
5. In the beginning was the _____.
8. __ johnson wrote this puzzle, (5.30.08).
11. _____, Isaac, and Jacob.
13. Thou shall not _____ .
17. (From 6 Down) . . . and my _____, (2Sam 22:3).
18. _____ and the door shall be opened.
19. (From 3 Down) . . . and my _____, (Ps 62:6).
21. '_____ of heaven', (a food).
23. My _____ know my voice.

Go For It Clues Continued:
Across:

24. First man.
25. True or False: Jacob was one of the twelve tribes.
29. Moab is his son, (Genesis 19:36-37).
31. The _____ commandments.
33. My_____ and I are one.
34. The _____ seduced Eve.
35. Jesus loves the little _____.
37. 'He who harms the _____ of mine does also to me.'
39. Let my people ____.
41. Like a _____ planted by the water.
42. Be still and _____ I am God.
44. A coat of many _____.
45. The _____ lights the night.
46. Noah had _____ sons.

Down:
2. Jesus loves ____.
3. The LORD is my _____, (to 19 Across).
4. His _____ endures to all generations.
6. He is my _____, (to 17 Across)
7. Also called Israel.
9. David's bosom buddy.
10. Considered too sacred to pronounce.
12. The children of Israel ate this during their 40 year trip in the desert.
14. Abraham's son, recognized by God as the one to receive his promise.
15. Son of God.
16. Do not depend on your own _____.
17. The LORD is my _____, (to 43 Down).
20. 'Let the people _____ thee O God,' (Psalm 67:3).
22. A man after God's heart.
23. God created the earth in _____ days.
25. God is our _____.
26. In all your ways _____ Him.
27. His wife was changed to a pillar of salt.
28. Garden of _____.
30. Jesus didn't come into the world to _____ it, (John 3:17).
32. The ____ rules the day.
33. It rained for _____ days and nights.
36. Not full.
38. The _____ was without form and void.
40. Honor thy father and _____.
43. (From 17 Down) . . . I shall not _____.

Goodness of the LORD
Various from Romans, the Psalms, KJV

(Note: Numbers read from left to right, whether clue is Across or Down.)

Across:

1. _____ to that which is good, (from Romans 12:9; alternate word).
3. Who is credited with writing the book of Romans?
5. The book of Psalms is not comprised of _____.
9. (Con't from 14 D) . . . knowledge of _____ and evil.
11. All have _____, (Romans. 3:23; Continued in 12 D)
13. Who makes it a struggle to do what is good?
15. Make a joyful _____, (Psalm 66:1).
17. _____ the LORD is good; (Continued 38 D)

Goodness Clues Continued:
Across:

18. Puzzle content designed by _____ (09.04.04).
19. Overcome _____ with good.
20. God considered everything that he _____ to be good, (Gen. 1:31).
22. A _____ can be a song, a chant, or the playing of an instrument.
23. The book of Psalms has more than _____ author.
25. Another word for dissimulation is _____, (Rom 12:9).
27. For I know that in me, dwells no _____ thing.
29. We did not, could not have made _____.
36. Adam and Eve were permitted to _____ of anything in the garden, (con't in 14 D).
37. The righteousness of God is by faith in _____ _____, (2 words; Rom 3:22)
39. In Biblical times, Rome was an _____.
40. We are the _____ of his pasture, (Ps 100:3).
42. _____ is the measure of all things good.
43. _____ is credited with penning seventy-three of the Psalms.
44. For what I want _____, I don't do, (2 wds; see Rom 7:15), (to 28D).
45. Be thankful unto Him and _____ his name.

Down:

2. Enter into his _____ with . . . (to 7 D).
4. Paul, who penned Romans, was an _____.
6. (Con't from 10 Down), It is _____ who hath made us and not . . . ; (Ps 100:3) (see 29A).
7. (From 2 Down), _____; and . . . ; (to 41 D).
8. The _____ that dwells in me is the cause of me doing that which I do.
10. _____ ye that the LORD he is God, (Ps 100:3) (to 6D).
11. Come before his presence with _____, Ps 100:2.
12. (From 11A) . . . and _____ short of the glory of God.
14. (From 36 A) . . . except the fruit from the _____ of . . . ; (Con't in 9A) (Gen 2:17).
16. (From 35 D) . . . and, I know my _____, (John 10:14).
21. _____ that which is evil (Rom 12:9).
24. Praise is what __ __, (2 wds), (Ps 119:164).
26. Do not let evil _____ you, (Rom 12:21).
28. (From 44A) . . . but that which I _____ want to do is what I do anyway.
30. Paul was known as _____ in his younger days.
31. Let _____ be without dissimulation, (Rom 12:19).
32. (From 38 D) and his _____ endures to all generations, (Ps 100:5).
33. An epistle is a _____.
34. How can we _____ that which is good without being taught?(Rom 7:18).
35. I am the good _____, (con't in 16D)
38. (From 17A) . . . his _____ is everlasting; (Continued in 32D)
41. (From 7 D) . . . into his courts with _____, (Ps 100:4).

Grow In Christ
1 Peter 2; KJV

(Note: Numbers read left to right, line by line, whether clue is Across or Down; also number of spaces in a clue does not always match number of spaces in the answer.)

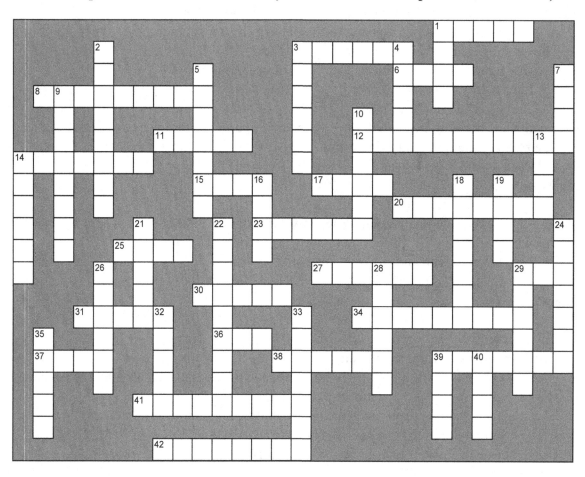

Across:

1. God's people have obtained _____.
3. Peter wrote that Christ's followers are living _____.
6. God's people are a special people; a _____ nation.
8. Christians are to offer up _____ sacrifices.
11. We must submit ourselves to every ordinance of man for the _____ sake.
12. Tasted in verse 3 refers to _____.
14. Christian must be mindful of the rule of _____ where they live.
15. This word is used often to portray respect and reverence.
17. The cross is depicted as a _____.
20. Watchful guarding and resentful suspicions are traits of _____.
23. The chief cornerstone: _____.

Grow In Christ Clues Continued:
Across:

25. We must do everything as unto the _____.
27. A _____ is an overseer.
29. Honor all _____.
30. God's chosen are considered a _____ priesthood.
31. Froward in verse 18 can be translated as: to be _____.
34. His light is designated as _____.
36. Be subject to good bosses, and even _____ so good bosses.
37. _____ the brotherhood.
38. Peter said that before God called us we were not a _____.
39. Servants are _____ to their masters.
41. An _____ can be described as being an institution.
42. Jesus is described in verse 25 as the _____.

Down:

1. We grow by the sincere _____ of the Word.
2. God called us out of _____ into His amazing light.
3. We are to _____ to the ordinance of men.
4. Before we accepted Christ as savior, we were like _____ gone astray.
5. Gentiles will _____ God when they see the good works of Christians.
7. The Lord is _____.
9. We were chosen to _____ the praises of God.
10. Guile is the same as _____.
13. Feeling discontent for what someone else has; wishing it were yours: _____.
14. Jesus Christ suffered, so shall we ____.
16. Peter's name translates as _____.
18. Malice is _____ (2 wds).
19. Sincere in verse 2 alludes to _____.
21. When we do as God asks, we silence the ignorance of _____.
22. This puzzle designed by _____, (Nov. 30, 2007).
24. Conversation is used here to mean _____.
26. To be buffeted is to be _____.
28. We are _____ of our sin by the stripes Jesus endured upon his body.
29. Used to specify or address a teacher.
32. Love, _____, respect.
33. To be a hypocrite is to _____ to be something you are not.
35. Christ gave his _____ as a sacrifice for our sins.
39. Jesus bore our _____ in His body.
40. New Christians are often referred to as _____ Christians.

How Much Do I Really Know
Various KJV Scriptures

Clues:

Jesus rose from grave after ___ days

Joshua was a type of ____

David had several _____ ; so did Solomon

Not our ___ but yours O Lord

The first child of David & Bathsheba

____ and morning star

A ____ to cool the day

Ark of the _____

She cut off Samson's hair

Immanuel also spelled _____

Samson's strength was in his ____

The walls of ____ fell down

An important river for Israel

David ____ Bathsheba's husband

_____, and the door shall be opened

He who has an ear let him ___

A best friend of David

Tender _____

Loving-_____

Thrown out of heaven

A ____ of fire for direction at night

Secondary wives

A harlot and an ancestor of Jesus

Before the flood there was no ____

A ____ of the angels joined Satan

Delilah seduced ____

____ is a devil

Satan was an ____

Rose of ____

His wives turned his heart

Times marched around Jericho

David's son, also king of Israel

Solomon loved _____ women

Israel lived in ____ in the desert

_____ were descendants of Levi

Lead us not into ____

First husband of Bathsheba

From the _____ of the sun

Saul was envious of _____

Puzzle by _____ (04.18.08)

How Much Do I Really Know
Various Scripture, KJV

Figure out what words the clues represent, then circle the words in the grid. Words can go across, down and in three diagonals. You may even find unscripted words in the grid. It's all good.

```
Y  Y  J  C  S  R  D  C  O  V  E  N  A  N  T  H  A  I  R  L
T  Q  T  E  A  I  T  J  K  I  N  D  N  E  S  S  C  R  R  D
G  M  V  H  E  P  R  K  O  P  H  K  K  R  C  X  Z  L  C  A
C  I  A  D  Y  I  L  H  G  N  T  L  N  I  I  H  G  Z  W  V
W  B  C  C  N  L  W  V  L  H  A  O  W  L  L  S  R  F  N  I
D  Z  P  I  J  L  C  M  G  P  M  T  L  F  P  L  I  I  B  D
K  C  A  P  E  A  S  I  T  O  R  I  H  S  P  K  E  N  S  N
W  R  L  A  R  R  E  L  K  W  I  A  A  T  Q  S  D  G  T
R  J  F  N  I  B  B  O  V  P  T  T  E  H  N  T  T  K  K
W  N  N  G  C  K  S  Y  M  E  A  H  I  S  R  L  E  J  C  T
L  K  G  E  H  F  M  T  E  N  N  R  R  A  T  S  M  J  O  P
G  U  Q  L  O  N  K  H  R  M  D  K  N  E  T  S  P  O  C  D
H  W  C  V  M  N  V  W  C  R  C  G  M  N  E  L  T  H  U  L
Q  Z  D  I  O  R  Y  B  Y  O  E  K  E  B  S  C  A  N  B  K
Q  K  K  S  F  R  D  N  N  L  Z  T  X  H  L  L  T  S  I  W
R  C  M  D  R  E  M  K  N  J  C  W  A  O  X  R  I  O  N  M
K  A  Y  M  W  X  R  H  E  A  R  R  U  F  Q  G  O  N  E  T
S  R  D  E  L  I  L  A  H  K  O  D  M  L  M  W  N  N  S  H
E  M  M  A  N  U  E  L  T  N  X  U  R  I  A  H  K  P  D  X
J  O  R  D  A  N  D  G  P  S  O  L  O  M  O  N  Q  C  X  R
```

Israel's Only Redeemer, So Says Isaiah
Isaiah 1:1; 43:1-19, KJV

(Note: Numbers read left to right, line by line, whether clue is Across or Down; also number of spaces in a clue does not always match number of spaces in the answer.)

Across:

2. Israel was chosen to be God's _ _ _ _ _ _.
4. God said that He had created Israel for His _ _ _ _ _.
9. This place is uninhabited.
10. 'Bring forth the _ _ _ _ _ people, . . .'(to 39D).
11. God said he gave this country for the ransom of Israel.
13. 'Behold, I will do a new _ _ _ _ _.'
15. 'I have declared, and _ _ _ _ _, and I have proclaimed.'
16. Seba was a son of _ _ _ _ and a grandson of Ham.
20. Sons and _ _ _ _ _ _ will come from all places of the earth.
23. God chose Babylon to _ _ _ _ _ _ Israel, (to 28A).
24. Israel is the seed or house of _ _ _ _.

Israel's Redeemer Clues Continued:
Across:

28. (From 23A) . . . , but _ _ _ _ _ _ will be brought down as fugitives, (to 3D).
30. A common occurrence throughout this passage is God telling Israel, 'I _ _.'
31. God promised to make rivers in the _ _ _ _ _ _.
34. The number of books written determine if a prophet is a _ _ _ _ _, prophet, (to 44A).
36. The name of this country translates as Cush which means black.
38. Author of Isaiah _ _ _ _ _.
40. _ _ _ _ (all caps) in the OT translates as Jehovah.
41. "I have called thee by thy _ _ _ _."
42. There was no God _ _ _ _ _ Jehovah, nor will there be one after him.
43. The Holy One of _ _ _ _ _ _.
44. (From 34A) . . . , or if he is considered a _ _ _ _ _ prophet.
45. The father of Isaiah.

Down:

1. 'I am the LORD thy _ _ _.'
2. God said He would bring their _ _ _ _ from the east, west, north, and south.
3. (From 28A) . . . , along with the Chaldeans who trusts in their _ _ _ _ _.
5. God reminded Israel that He _ _ _ _ _ them.
6. God declared, "I am your _ _ _ _."
7. Isaiah was a _ _ _ _ _ _ _.
8. 'Fear _ _ _.'
12. 'Let them hear and say, 'It is _ _ _ _ _.'
14. Egypt is translated as Mitsrayim who was a son of _ _ _ _.
17. It is said that this king sawed Isaiah into pieces, (2Ki 21:16; Heb 11:37).
18. Isaiah's vision concerned this group of the original tribes, and Israel.
19. God wanted Israel to be a _ _ _ _ _ _ _ of him to other nations.
21. God loved his chosen so much, He _ _ _ _ men for them.
22. Isaiah had the ear of both the priestly leadership and the _ _ _ _ _ palace.
24. Isaiah was a citizen of this city.
25. God declared himself as the _ _ _ _ _ _ _ of Israel.
26. (From 32D) . . . , 'When you walk through the fire, you will not be _ _ _ _ _ _.'
27. God reminded his people that they were _ _ _ _ _ _ _ _ _ in his sight.
29. 'Remember _ _ _ _ the former things.'
32. 'I will be with thee through the _ _ _ _ _ _,' (to 26D).
33. 'There is _ _ _ _ that can deliver you from my hand.'
35. Puzzle written by tj _ _ _ _ _ _ _ _ _, (05/31/04).
37. The LORD said to Israel, 'thou art _ _ _ _, (see 33D).
39. (From 10A) '. . . and the _ _ _ _ that have ears.'

Jesus, According To John
John 1:1-34, KJV

(Note: Numbers read from left to right, whether clue is Across or Down)

Jesus, According To John Clues:
Across:

3. In the Beginning was the _ _ _ _.
6. _ _ _ _ _ gives or provides authority.
7. John's writing is one of four referred to as the _ _ _ _ _ _.
8. _ _ _ is this man, Jesus?
10. The _ _ _ _ was in the beginning with God.
13. John, the writer, and his brother partnered with _ _ _ _ _ and his brother, (Lk. 5:10).
14. We must believe in and on His _ _ _ _.
16. The man John mentioned in this narrative had a title of 'the _ _ _ _ _ _.'
19. Jesus is called the only _ _ _ _ _ _ _ _ son.
22. This chapter speaks of a man sent from God named _ _ _ _.
23. John, the writer, said, "I saw the Spirit descending from heaven like a _ _ _ _.
24. The Word was _ _ _ _ God.
25. (Cont from 5 Down) but _ _ _ _ _ and truth comes by Jesus Christ.
27. No man has seen God at any _ _ _ _.
29. His own did not _ _ _ _ _ _ _ him.
31. _ _ the Beginning
32. Preferred before also means _ _ _ _ _ higher, (present tense).
33. God's children are _ _ _ _ of him.
37. Greek translation for 'word'.
39. His life is called the _ _ _ _ _ of men.
41. "In Him is _ _ _ _."
42. This puzzle content created by _ _ johnson, (11.28.02).
44. He gave the right to believers to become _ _ _ _ or children of God.
45. John was a witness for one who would come _ _ _ _ _ him.
46. _ _ _ things were made by him.
48. Nothing that was made was made without _ _ _.
50. The father and the son are _ _ _.
51. Those who _ _ _ _ _ _ _ _ on or in his name received something special, (past tense).

Down:

1. John writes that Jesus is in the _ _ _ _ _ of the Father.
2. Grace and truth came by _ _ _ _ _ Christ.
4. (Con't from 35 Down) . . . , and _ _ _ _ _ among us, (past tense).
5. The law was given by _ _ _ _ _ . . . , (to 25 Across).
6. John's mission was to _ _ _ _ _ _ _ _ the way for Jesus Christ.
9. Jesus is the _ _ _ of God.

Jesus, According To John, Down Clues Continued:

11. The light of Jesus is the _ _ _ _ light.
12. John, the writer, had a brother named _ _ _ _ _.
15. John was one of the _ _ _ _ _ _ who was given the great commission from Jesus before He ascended into heaven (Mark 16:14-18; Acts 1:6-26).
17. John and his brother were called sons of _ _ _ _ _ _ _, (Mark 3:17).
18. The world _ _ _ _ _ _ know Him (2 wds).
20. The father is full of grace and _ _ _ _ _.
21. God is our _ _ _ _ _ _.
24. John was sent to bear _ _ _ _ _ _ _ of the light.
25. We beheld his _ _ _ _ _.
26. The darkness did/does not _ _ _ _ _ _ _ _ _ _ the light of God.
28. The Light directs the way of every _ _ _ (or person) that comes into the world.
30. John of the story declared, "I am not the _ _ _ _ _ _."
34. It is necessary to distinguish things which are true from things which are _ _ _ _ _.
35. The Word was made _ _ _ _ _ _ . . . , (to 4 Down).
36. John, the writer, was a _ _ _ _ _ _ _ _ _ before he was called to follow Jesus.
38. The work of Jesus _ _ _ _ _ _ _ the Father, (present tense).
40. The _ _ _ _ _ and everything in it was made by God.
43. John reminded us that He who would come after him would be preferred _ _ _ _ _ _ him.
46. I _ _.
47. John, the writer, is said to be the disciple that Jesus _ _ _ _ _.
49. John writes, "The Word was _ _ _."

Bible Reading for Nicodemus, John 3:1-21, KJV
Puzzle on Page 38-39:

1) "There was a man of the Pharisees, named Nicodemus, a ruler of the Jews:
2) The same came to Jesus by night, and said unto him, Rabbi, we know that thou art a teacher come from God: for no man can do these miracles that thou doest, except God be with him.
3) Jesus answered and said unto him, Verily, verily, I say unto thee, Except a man be born again, he cannot see the kingdom of God.
4) Nicodemus said unto him, How can a man be born when he is old? can he enter the second time into his mother's womb, and be born?"

Nicodemus Reading Continued, John 3:1-21, KJV:
(Puzzle on Page 38-39)

5) "Jesus answered, Verily, verily, I say unto thee, Except a man be born of water and [of] the Spirit, he cannot enter into the kingdom of God.

6) That which is born of the flesh is flesh; and that which is born of the Spirit is spirit.

7) Marvel not that I said unto thee, Ye must be born again.

8) The wind bloweth where it listeth, and thou hearest the sound thereof, but canst not tell whence it cometh, and whither it goeth: so is every one that is born of the Spirit.

9) Nicodemus answered and said unto him, How can these things be?

10) Jesus answered and said unto him, Art thou a master of Israel, and knowest not these things?

11) Verily, verily, I say unto thee, We speak that we do know, and testify that we have seen; and ye receive not our witness.

12) If I have told you earthly things, and ye believe not, how shall ye believe, if I tell you [of] heavenly things?

13) And no man hath ascended up to heaven, but he that came down from heaven, [even] the Son of man which is in heaven.

14) And as Moses lifted up the serpent in the wilderness, even so must the Son of man be lifted up:

15) That whosoever believeth in him should not perish, but have eternal life.

16) For God so loved the world, that he gave his only begotten Son, that whosoever believeth in him should not perish, but have everlasting life.

17) For God sent not his Son into the world to condemn the world; but that the world through him might be saved.

18) He that believeth on him is not condemned: but he that believeth not is condemned already, because he hath not believed in the name of the only begotten Son of God.

19) And this is the condemnation, that light is come into the world, and men loved darkness rather than light, because their deeds were evil.

20) For every one that doeth evil hateth the light, neither cometh to the light, lest his deeds should be reproved.

21) But he that doeth truth cometh to the light, that his deeds may be made manifest, that they are wrought in God."

Jesus And Nicodemus
John 3:1-21, KJV

Across Clues:

4. Verses printed in red normally refer to words that _____ spoke.
5. To be _____ in God, suggests that a Christian's deeds are implemented, or performed in God.
7. The concept of rebirth, according to Jesus, is of the _____, (see also 9D).
8. Israel is synonymous with the _____.
11. He wanted to know how the things Jesus told him could be.
12. Ye _____ be born again.
14. '____ speak that which we know.'
15. Nicodemus was considered a _____ of the Jews.
19. Jesus came into the world so that the world could be _____.
20. Translates as: surely, truly, or indeed.
22. By calling Jesus _____ conceded that Jesus must have been sent by God.
24. Jesus did not come to earth to _____ the earth.
26. 'The Son of man must be _____ up.'
31. Anyone who does not believe in Jesus is condemned _____.
32. If you don't believe earthly things, how will you believe _____ things?
33. ____ love darkness rather than light.
34. 'That which is born of the _____ is flesh; . . .'
35. A _____ is also known as a teacher.
36. Anyone who _____ in Jesus is not condemned.
39. Moses lifted up a _____ serpent in the wilderness.
40. Nicodemus came to see Jesus during the _____.
41. There are certain requirements before one can enter into God's _____.
42. Reproved in verse 20 means _____.
43. This term defines Jesus as one of a kind.

Down:

1. Our _____ are made known when we come into the light.
2. You receive not ____ witness.
3. Nicodemus was a _____.
6. . . . that which is born of the _____ is spirit.
9. Jesus declared that a man must be born of both _____ and (see 7A).
10. Except a man be _____ again . . . , (see 41A).
12. This puzzle content was _____ by tjjohnson, (02.11.05).
13. God so _____ the world.
14. The _____ blows where it wishes.
16. The deeds of man are _____.
17. Accepting the _____ brings one into the light.
18. Nicodemus wanted to know how a man could be born again when he is _____.
19. The ____ of man will ascend back into heaven.

Down Clues Continued:

21. _____ created Jesus.

23. This word in verse three refers to 'from above'.

25. _____ so.

27. Rabbi is a title used when addressing a _____.

28. The question was asked whether a man could go back into his mother's ____.

29. Whosoever believes in Jesus will have eternal ____.

30. Whosoever believes in Jesus shall not _____.

35. Jesus reminded Nicodemus that he was known as a _____ of Israel.

37. Those who practice evil, hates the _____.

38. This word is Greek for verily.

**Jesus And Nicodemus,
John 3:1-21, KJV**

(Note: Numbers go from left to right, line by line, whether clue is Across or Down)

Jesus The Greater, John The Lesser, Matthew 3, KJV

Puzzle Clues:

The Jews called him their father

John _____ all the people of the area

This is my _____ Son

John's _____ were made of camel's hair

Jesus and John the Baptist were _____

Unproductive trees are (2 words)

Spirit of God descended like a _____

A belt is described as a _____

The _____ opened after Jesus was baptized

Prophet in verse three

The Kingdom of Heaven refers to _____

He baptized with the Holy Ghost

The area where John preached was _____

His food was wild honey and _____.

Interpreters of the law

Voice from heaven said I am well _____.

To _____ is to have a sincere change of mind and attitude

Baptism of Jesus fulfilled all _____

Had doubts of Jesus' teaching

John didn't feel worthy to carry Jesus' _____

He baptized with water (2 words)

Author of this (8.18.2008) puzzle is _____

John the Baptist felt _____ to baptize Jesus

The lawmakers were referred to as _____

A _____ spoke from heaven

Loins refers to John's _____

John was said to be as 'a voice crying in the _____'

Jesus The Greater--John, The Lesser
Matthew 3, KJV

Figure out what words the clues on the previous page represent, then circle the words in the grid. Words can go across, down and in three diagonals. You may find unscripted words in the puzzle grid.

```
W  R  I  G  H  T  E  O  U  S  N  E  S  S  V  D  T  M  X  S
C  M  M  T  T  H  E  B  A  P  T  I  S  T  W  D  O  V  E  A
R  B  Z  R  X  H  T  R  D  T  R  P  R  V  F  L  X  Z  G  D
C  P  V  I  P  E  R  S  D  N  D  M  H  R  W  K  Z  B  F  D
M  L  R  M  C  L  O  T  H  E  S  B  R  A  W  P  Z  V  W  U
S  E  N  D  B  L  S  J  Z  W  I  L  D  E  R  N  E  S  S  C
H  A  K  V  M  N  C  I  T  H  J  W  M  M  J  I  C  M  G  E
O  S  K  G  I  L  T  J  L  E  T  P  L  C  Q  E  S  V  Z  E
E  E  B  S  T  P  J  J  S  D  R  N  P  L  N  T  S  E  M  S
S  D  U  W  A  O  D  U  Q  L  E  F  L  N  D  X  D  U  E  H
N  O  D  B  H  J  S  Y  V  W  P  L  T  T  J  Z  C  M  S  S
C  C  R  N  T  F  U  S  B  N  E  W  O  R  T  Z  G  J  K  Z
X  G  S  Q  T  V  N  D  W  Y  N  B  R  C  H  M  U  R  V  Z
Y  O  M  L  H  E  G  O  E  R  T  P  E  A  U  N  M  A  R  W
N  M  T  N  V  Q  D  G  L  A  L  M  I  L  W  S  B  J  W  B
K  G  P  A  E  T  V  I  X  R  D  A  L  O  O  R  T  A  P  R
G  T  E  C  U  P  H  R  L  H  S  K  R  Y  A  V  I  X  M  H
P  H  I  C  K  P  L  D  N  I  K  T  D  H  G  S  E  H  W  G
L  O  N  R  T  K  W  L  T  B  H  N  A  V  T  N  R  D  N  L
V  K  Q  K  Y  Q  Y  E  T  Y  V  M  T  M  M  D  J  N  R  M
```

41

Jesus, The Son of David
Matthew 1; 9:9-10, KJV

(Numbers read from left to right, line by line, whether clue is Across or Down; also number of spaces in a clue does not always match number of spaces in the answer.)

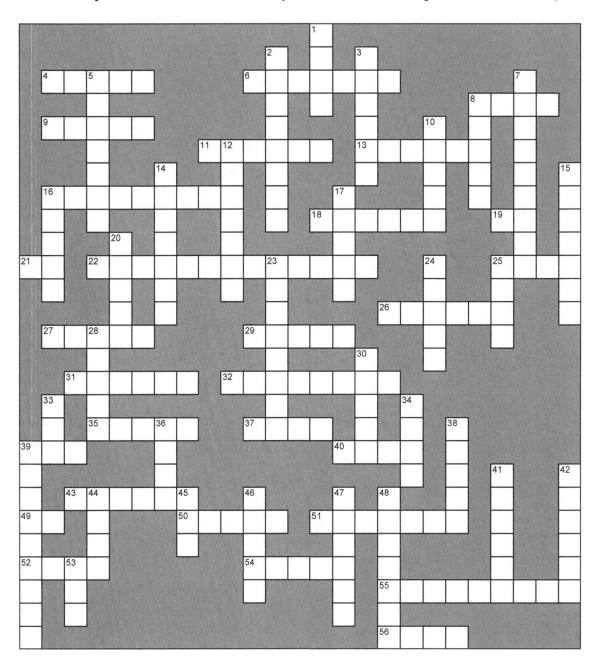

Jesus, The Son of David Clues:
Across:

4. Which son of Jacob carries on the heritage of Jesus?
6. Jesus came to _ _ _ _ _ _ _ that which was prophesied.
8. Pharez was a great grandfather (many times over) of _ _ _ _, (Ruth 4:18-21).
9. Abraham is listed in the lineage of Jesus as the son of _ _ _ _ _.
11. The literal translation of the name Jesus as used in verse 21 is _ _ _ _ _ _ _.
13. Jesus was accused of _ _ _ _ _ _ with sinners.
16. Even though he was of the family of Joseph, and a king, he did not have a descendant to sit on the throne of David, (2 Ki. 24:8; Jer. 22:24-30).
18. Jacob begat the _ _ _ _ _ _ of Israel.
19. Jesus said to Matthew, "follow _ _."
21. Did Mary name her son?
22. Pharez's mother was Judah's _ _ _ _ _ _, (Gen 38:11), (could be hyphenated).
25. ". . . for he shall _ _ _ _ his people . . ." (to 25D).
26. Mary was a _ _ _ _ _ _ mother . . . , (to 27A).
27. (Continued from 26A) . . . , and a virgin _ _ _ _ _.
29. She was the mother of Boaz.
31. Rahab/Rachab, a _ _ _ _ _ _ _, was great-grandmother (many times over) of David.
32. Matthew segmented the genealogy of Jesus into groups of _ _ _ _ _ _ _.
35. "Behold a virgin shall be with _ _ _ _ _ . . . ;"
37. Joseph's father was _ _ _ _ named Jacob.
39. "_ _ _ she shall bring forth a son . . ."
40. It is said that the lineage of Jesus was proven for the benefit of the _ _ _.
43. 'The book of the generation of Jesus _ _ _ _ _ _ . . .'
49. The birth of Jesus was _ _ this wise: (v18).
50. An _ _ _ _ _ convinced Joseph to go ahead and marry Mary.
51. Joseph was called the _ _ _ _ _ _ _ of Mary when they became espoused, (v19).
52. Which of Judah's wives gave birth to Pharez?
54. Joseph and Mary did not consummate their marriage _ _ _ _ _ after she gave birth to Jesus.
55. Mary was with child of the _ _ _ _ _ _ _ _ _ _ (2 wds.).
56. The mother of Jesus.

Down:

1. The only mention of Mary in Jesus' genealogy is as Joseph's _ _ _ _.
2. A name for Matthew's official position.
3. Some forefathers of Jesus were born as _ _ _ _ _ _ in captivity.

(Down Clues Continued Next Page)

Jesus, Son of David Clues Continued:
Down:

5. For Joseph to put Mary away was similar to a _ _ _ _ _ _ _.
7. An ancestor of Jesus and the wife of Uriah.
8. The same means to father a child.
10. David, Solomon, Jehoshaphat, Uzziah, and Hezekiah were known as _ _ _ _ _.
12. Joseph was _ _ _ _ _ _ _ for Mary's condition.
14. Mary was _ _ _ _ _ _ _ to Joseph when she became pregnant with Jesus.
15. This puzzle _ _ _ _ _ _ _ was created by tj johnson,(12.30.04) .
16. Isaac begat _ _ _ _ _.
17. The angel spoke to Joseph in a _ _ _ _ _ .
20. Jesus was born a descendant to the throne of _ _ _ _ _ _.
23. The title given to Mary's baby meaning 'God with us.'
24. Jesus was the _ _ _ _ _ born of Mary.
25. (Cont from 25Across) ". . . from their _ _ _ _.
28. Abraham begat _ _ _ _ _ _.
30. Boaz and Ruth were the grandparents of David's father, _ _ _ _ _.
33. She shall bring forth a _ _ _.
34. Joseph was considered a _ _ _ _ man.
36. The _ _ _ _ of betrothal were as binding as a marriage.
38. Ruth was the great-grandmother of _ _ _ _ _, (Ruth 4:10, 18-22).
39. Greek translation for Christ is _ _ _ _ _ _ _.
41. The ancestral lineage described in Matthew follows that of the husband of Mary, who was _ _ _ _ _ _.
42. The Holy Ghost is synonymous with the term Holy _ _ _ _ _ _.
44. Joseph thought he should _ _ _ _ Mary because of her condition.
45. Matthew was a _ _ _ collector.
46. Mary's baby was to be named _ _ _ _ _.
47. Joseph did not want to make Mary a _ _ _ _ _ _ example by breaking their vows of engagement.
48. Matthew began the lineage of Jesus from _ _ _ _ _ _ _.
53. Scripture says Joseph "knew her _ _ _ ."

King Herod Plots to Kill King Jesus
Matthew 2, KJV

"**1)** Now when Jesus was born in Bethlehem of Judaea in the days of Herod the king, behold, there came wise men from the east to Jerusalem, **2)** Saying, Where is he that is born King of the Jews? for we have seen his star in the east, and are come to worship him. **3)** When Herod the king had heard [these things], he was troubled, and all Jerusalem with him. **4)** And when he had gathered all the chief priests and scribes of the people together, he demanded of them where Christ should be born. **5)** And they said unto him, In Bethlehem of Judaea: for thus it is written by the prophet, **6)** And thou Bethlehem, [in] the land of Juda, art not the least among the princes of Juda: for out of thee shall come a Governor, that shall rule my people Israel. **7)** Then Herod, when he had privily called the wise men, enquired of them diligently what time the star appeared.

8) And he sent them to Bethlehem, and said, Go and search diligently for the young child; and when ye have found [him], bring me word again, that I may come and worship him also. **9)** When they had heard the king, they departed; and, lo, the star, which they saw in the east, went before them, till it came and stood over where the young child was. **10)** When they saw the star, they rejoiced with exceeding great joy. **11)** And when they were come into the house, they saw the young child with Mary his mother, and fell down, and worshipped him: and when they had opened their treasures, they presented unto him gifts; gold, and frankincense, and myrrh. **12)** And being warned of God in a dream that they should not return to Herod, they departed into their own country another way.

13) And when they were departed, behold, the angel of the Lord appeared to Joseph in a dream, saying, Arise, and take the young child and his mother, and flee into Egypt, and be thou there until I bring thee word: for Herod will seek the young child to destroy him. **14)** When he arose, he took the young child and his mother by night, and departed into Egypt: **15)** And was there until the death of Herod: that it might be fulfilled which was spoken of the Lord by the prophet, saying, Out of Egypt have I called my son. **16)** Then Herod, when he saw that he was mocked of the wise men, was exceeding wroth, and sent forth, and slew all the children that were in Bethlehem, and in all the coasts thereof, from two years old and under, according to the time which he had diligently enquired of the wise men. **17)** Then was fulfilled that which was spoken by Jeremy the prophet, saying, **18)** In Rama was there a voice heard, lamentation, and weeping, and great mourning, Rachel weeping [for] her children, and would not be comforted, because they are not. **19)** But when Herod was dead, behold, an angel of the Lord appeared in a dream to Joseph in Egypt, **20)** Saying, Arise, and take the young child and his mother, and go into the land of Israel: for they are dead which sought the young child's life. **21)** And he arose, and took the young child and his mother, and came into the land of Israel. **22)** But when he heard that Archelaus did reign in Judaea in the room of his father Herod, he was afraid to go thither: notwithstanding, being warned of God in a dream, he turned aside into the parts of Galilee: **23)** And he came and dwelt in a city called Nazareth: that it might be fulfilled which was spoken by the prophets, He shall be called a Nazarene."

King Herod Plots to Kill King Jesus,
Matthew 2, KJV

Across Clues:
1. The wise men followed a _____ from the east.
3. The prophet quoted in verse 15.
5. He was also warned in a dream about Herod.
9. Governor, or _____.
10. Herod wanted to set the time of the 'star' to estimate when Jesus was ____.
12. Hebrew translation is 'House of Bread'
15. _____ warned the wise men not to return to Herod.
16. Verse 18 identifies the _____ of Israel.
17. Jesus is not a _____ in this story.
19. Children (v16) refers to _____ children.
21. Content created by _____, (05.10.2003).
26. King Herod didn't want to worship Jesus, he wanted to kill or _____ him.
27. He was troubled about the status of the newborn king.
30. The young child Jesus was taken to _____ by his parents.
33. Interpreters of the law.
34. Chief priests or _____ priests.
35. The prophet referred to in verse 5.
36. _____ is called the home town of Jesus.
37. The father of Israel; also called Israel.
38. Mocked, as used in verse 16.
39. Bethlehem is located in the land of _____.

Down:
1. Privately, privily, or _____.
2. Bethlehem is located near _____.
4. _____ reigned after his father Herod.
6. Jesus was born about ____ years before Herod began his murderous search.
7. Jesus was born King of the _____.
8. An angel of the _____.
11. Jeremiah prophesied about _____ weeping for her children.
13. The wise men also called _____.
14. Angry or anger, verse 16.
16. In this story, Jesus is called the _____.
18. A young child.
20. Another name for Bethlehem, (Gen 35:19).
22. The gifts brought to Jesus included gold, frankincense, and _____.
23. To rule in verse 6 describes 'to feed, keep, or _____.'
24. King Herod known as Herod the _____

King Herod Clues Down Continued:

25. When they saw the young Jesus, they _____ him.
28. Joseph was advised to return to Israel when Herod _____ .
29. When wise men saw the star hover over where Jesus was, they _____ .
31. Herod sent the _____ in search of Jesus, (2 wds).
32. Instead of going back to his home, Joseph went to the region of _____ when he discovered that Archelaus reigned in Judaea.

King Herod Plots to Kill King Jesus
Matthew 2, KJV

(Note: Numbers read left to right, whether clue is Across or Down)

Letter To Galatians-1
Galatians 1, KJV

Clues Across:

3. Before Paul was converted he _ _ _ _ _ _ _ _ the church.
5. This puzzle content created by _ _ johnson, (03.25.05).
7. Jesus gave himself as a sacrifice to forgive our _ _ _ _.
8. The meeting between Jesus and Saul happened during a trip on the _ _ _ _ to Damascus.
11. Paul claimed that his profession of the faith was not made by _ _ _.
12. 'When it _ _ _ _ _ _ _ God . . .' (v15)
14. Judean refers to the area named after the tribe of _ _ _ _ _ _.
15. Being unknown by _ _ _ _ to the churches of Judea, Paul was still welcomed there.
17. Paul proclaimed himself to be an _ _ _ _ _ _.
18. In these passages, world refers to _ _ _ _.
20. Before he was renamed Paul, he was _ _ _ _ _.
22. A familiar greeting of Paul's began with '_ _ _ _ _ [be] to you . . .
23. Verse eight claims that if any other _ _ _ _ _ _ is preached, it is accursed.
25. He who once persecuted us, now preaches the _ _ _ _ _.
27. The Greek translation for letter.
30. The gospel came to Paul by _ _ _ _ _ _ _ _ _ _ of Jesus Christ.
32. James, the Lord's _ _ _ _ _.
33. In the _ _ _ _ _ _ religion, Paul was favored above many his senior.
34. Paul accused some men of wanting to _ _ _ _ _ _ _ the gospel of Christ.
35. The Galatian letter was intended for the _ _ _ _ _ _ of that area.
36. God calls us by his _ _ _ _ _, as he did Paul.
37. Before his conversion, Paul said he _ _ _ _ _ the church, meaning he tried to destroy it.

Down:

1. Paul was concerned that the new Christian converts had _ _ _ _ _ _ away from the gospel of Christ.
2. The name of the city of the Galatians.
4. The Greek word for accursed is _ _ _ _ _.
6. An apostle that Paul visited in Jerusalem in his 4th year of apostleship was _ _ _ _.
9. Jesus Christ is _ _ _ in the form of a man.
10. Paul described himself as being more _ _ _ _ _ _ than many of his peers.
12. After three years, Paul went to Jerusalem to see _ _ _ _ _ _.
13. After being called to the gospel of Christ, Paul traveled to an area of _ _ _ _ _ _.
14. He gave himself for our sins, (2 words).
16. The Greek word for anointed is _ _ _ _ _.
19. Paul repeatedly states that he did not, and would not seek to _ _ _ _ _ _ men.
21. Heathen refers to _ _ _ _ _.

Letter To Galatians-1 Clues Continued:
Down:

23. Paul is known to write a lengthy _ _ _ _ _ _ _ _ in his letters.
24. Who wrote the letter to the Galatians?
26. Conversation in verse 13 refers to _ _ _ _ _.
28. Paul was called to _ _ _ _ _ the gospel to the Gentiles.
29. God's _ _ _ was revealed in Paul, according to Paul's letter.
31. Paul declared that after his conversion, he did not confer with flesh and _ _ _ _ _.

Letter To Galatians-1
Galatians 1, KJV

(Numbers read from left to right, line by line, whether clue is Across or Down; also number of spaces in a clue does not always match number of spaces in the answer.)

Letter To Galatians-2
Galatians 2, KJV

Galatian-2 Clues Across:

1. Paul and Barnabas received the _ _ _ _ _ hand of fellowship from the brethren.
4. Titus was a _ _ _ _ _, therefore a Gentile.
6. If we are as Paul, we have been _ _ _ _ _ with Christ.
9. The context of Paul's message for Galatia was that salvation is not of the _ _ _ _.
12. This cannot save anyone.
14. A constant companion of Paul's.
15. He had not been compelled to be circumcised as other converts had.
17. Called the apostle to the Gentiles.
18. The Jewish Christians in verses 11-14 were not walking according to the _ _ _ _.
20. Peter was not the only _ _ _ _ _ _ _ _ in how he acted at certain times, others behaved likewise.
21. Cephas, James, and John were referred to as _ _ _ _ _.
22. This word is used by Paul to indicate the Gentiles.
25. The opposite of freedom is _ _ _ _ _ _.
27. Man is justified by his faith in Jesus _ _ _ _ _ _.
31. _ _ _ _ _ _ _, a companion of Peter, was confused by the actions of the Jewish Christians.
32. Paul _ _ _ _ _ _ Peter for being wishy-washy, so to say.
33. Peter seemed to change his _ _ _ _ depending on where he was at the time.
35. Peter was influenced by _ _ _ _ _ _ in verse twelve.
38. One of the fellow travelers with Paul to Jerusalem was _ _ _ _ _ _.
40. Peter sometimes _ _ _ _ _ with the Gentiles.
42. To _ _ _ _ upright means to live according to the gospel of Christ.
43. Verse ten reminds us to remember the _ _ _ _ _.
45. One of Paul's main concerns in this passage is his _ _ _ _ _ _ _ converts.
46. Paul accused the Jewish spies of being _ _ _ _ _ _ _ of their Christian freedom.
47. Man is not _ _ _ _ _ _ _ _ _ by the works of the law.

Down:

2. Paul had _ _ _ _ _ with the way Peter acted when reputable Jews were present.
3. Faith in Jesus means you _ _ _ _ _ _ in Jesus.
5. Verse two says that Paul went to Jerusalem because of a _ _ _ _ _ _.
6. Refers to the Jews, (v7).

Down Clues Continued on Page 53:

Letter To Galatians-2
Galatians 2, KJV

(Note: Numbers read left to right, line by line, whether clue is Across or Down; also number of spaces not indicative of number of letters in the answer.)

Reading for Galatians 3, NKJV

1) "O foolish Galatians! Who has bewitched you that you should not obey the truth, before whose eyes Jesus Christ was clearly portrayed among you as crucified? **(2)** This only I want to learn from you: Did you receive the Spirit by the works of the law, or by the hearing of faith? **(3)** Are you so foolish? Having begun in the Spirit, are you now being made perfect by the flesh? **(4)** Have you suffered so many things in vain—if indeed it was in vain? **(5)** Therefore He who supplies the Spirit to you and works miracles among you, does He do it by the works of the law, or by the hearing of faith? **(6)** just as Abraham "believed God, and it was accounted to him for righteousness." **(7)** Therefore know that only those who are of faith are sons of Abraham. **(8)** And the Scripture, foreseeing that God would justify the Gentiles by faith, preached the gospel to Abraham beforehand, saying, "In you all the nations shall be blessed." **(9)** So then those who are of faith are blessed with believing Abraham. **(10)** For as many as are of the works of the law are under the curse; for it is written, "Cursed is everyone who does not continue in all things which are written in the book of the law, to do them." **(11)** But that no one is justified by the law in the sight of God is evident, for "the just shall live by faith." **(12)** Yet the law is not of faith, but "the man who does them shall live by them." **(13)** Christ has redeemed us from the curse of the law, having become a curse for us (for it is written, "Cursed is everyone who hangs on a tree"), **and (14)** that the blessing of Abraham might come upon the Gentiles in Christ Jesus, that we might receive the promise of the Spirit through faith. **(15)** Brethren, I speak in the manner of men: Though it is only a man's covenant, yet if it is confirmed, no one annuls or adds to it. **(16)** Now to Abraham and his Seed were the promises made. He does not say, "And to seeds," as of many, but as of one, "And to your Seed," who is Christ. **(17)** And this I say, that the law, which was four hundred and thirty years later, cannot annul the covenant that was confirmed before by God in Christ, that it should make the promise of no effect. **(18)** For if the inheritance is of the law, it is no longer of promise; but God gave it to Abraham by promise. **(19)** What purpose then does the law serve? It was added because of transgressions, till the Seed should come to whom the promise was made; and it was appointed through angels by the hand of a mediator. **(20)** Now a mediator does not mediate for one only, but God is one. **(21)** Is the law then against the promises of God? Certainly not! For if there had been a law given which could have given life, truly righteousness would have been by the law. **(22)** But the Scripture has confined all under sin, that the promise by faith in Jesus Christ might be given to those who believe. **(23)** But before faith came, we were kept under guard by the law, kept for the faith which would afterward be revealed. **(24)** Therefore the law was our tutor to bring us to Christ, that we might be justified by faith. **(25)** But after faith has come, we are no longer under a tutor. **(26)** For you are all sons of God through faith in Christ Jesus. **(27)** For as many of you as were baptized into Christ have put on Christ. **(28)** There is neither Jew nor Greek, there is neither slave nor free, there is neither male nor female; for you are all one in Christ Jesus. **(29)** And if you are Christ's, then you are Abraham's seed, and heirs according to the promise."

(Puzzle on Page 54)

Letter To Galatians-2, Continued from Page 50:
Down Clues,

7. The freedom that Christians have is/was made possible by _ _ _ _ _, (2 wds).

8. The gospel of Christ is _ _ _ _ _ _.

10. Peter, the _ _ _ _ _ _ to the Jews.

11. Contrary men seeking to find out what the Christians preached were referred to as _ _ _ _ _ brethren.

13. After his first trip to Jerusalem, Paul visited again _ _ _ _ _ years later.

16. The content of this puzzle created by _ _ johnson, (03.25.2005).

19. God gave us grace through the _ _ _ _ _ _ that his Son Jesus shed for us.

23. Jesus was nailed to a tree that was in the form of a _ _ _ _ _ _ _ _.

24. Some prominent among the Jews wanted the Gentile converts to be _ _ _ _ _ _ _ _ _ _.

26. At times Peter refrained from eating with Gentiles because he was _ _ _ _ _ of what influential Jews might do or say.

28. Paul wanted to take the gospel to the _ _ _ _ _ _, (v 9).

29. If righteousness is given by the law, then Christ died in _ _ _ _ _ _.

30. Cephas is the same as _ _ _ _ _.

32. Paul called Peter on his ambivalence _ _ _ _ _ everyone.

34. Verse two says that Paul preached to men of reputation _ _ _ _ _ _ _ _.

36. Gentiles were generally labeled as being _ _ _ _ _ _.

37. To be justified means we are made _ _ _ _ _ _.

39. God does not _ _ _ _ _ one person over another.

41. When Paul opposed Peter, he did so to his _ _ _ _ _.

44. The Gospel is the _ _ _ _ news or tidings of Jesus Christ.

Letter To Galatians-3
Galatians 3, KJV

Galatians-3 Clues Across:

2. The promise spoken of in verse nineteen was ordained by _ _ _ _ _.
6. The scripture says, 'Cursed is every one that hangeth on a _ _ _ _.'
7. The law cannot _ _ _ _ _ us.
8. Those who live according to the works of the law, are under a _ _ _ _ _ _.
12. Because of his belief, Abraham was made _ _ _ _ _ _ _.
13. The Galatians seemed to be _ _ _ _ _ _ about the law and faith.
15. The just shall _ _ _ _ by faith.
18. One does not receive the _ _ _ _ _ _ by the works of the law.
21. We are all _ _ _ in Christ.
23. Abraham _ _ _ _ _ _ _ _ God.
25. The blessing of Abraham comes to the _ _ _ _ _ _ through Jesus Christ.
26. Have you _ _ _ on Christ as Paul preached?
28. The promise was made to the _ _ _ _ of Abraham.
30. To _ _ _ _ _ _, the promised stated, 'In thee shall all nations be blessed.'
32. The Spirit comes by hearing of the _ _ _ _ _.
36. (From 43 D), 'promise by faith of Jesus Christ might be given to them that _ _ _ _ _ _.'
37. The _ _ _ _ _ _ to Abraham was given four hundred thirty years before the law.
39. The scripture says that God would _ _ _ _ _ _ the heathen through faith.
41. '_ _ _ _ _ _ be to God.'
44. _ _ you believe in Christ Jesus?
45. Paul feared that many of the Galatian Christians had suffered in _ _ _ _ _.
46. Those of faith are also _ _ _ _ _ _ _ _ of Abraham.
49. A letter and an epistle are the _ _ _ _ _.

Down:

1. Jesus was _ _ _ _ _ _ _ for the Galatians, just as he was for all of us.
3. The promise of (39 Across) was preached to Abraham, before the _ _ _ _ _ _.
4. Christ was made a curse for _ _ _ _ _.
5. If we believe, we are _ _ _ _ _ of the promise.
8. _ _ _ _ _ redeemed us from the curse of the law.
9. (From 14 D), Paul asked the Galatians, 'Who _ _ _ _ _ you?'
10. So those of faith are _ _ _ _ _ _ _ because Abraham believed.
11. We are all considered to be children of _ _ _ by faith.
14. Paul called the Galatian believers _ _ _ _ _, (continued in 9D).
16. _ _ _ _ _ is ultimately the seed of Abraham.
17. The gift of the Spirit is given to us by _ _ _ _ _ _.
19. This puzzle content created by _ _ johnson, (03.25.2005).
20. There is neither _ _ _ nor Greek.
22. There is neither male nor _ _ _ _ _.

Galatians 3 Down Clues Continued:

24. No man is _ _ _ _ _ _ by the works of the law, (to 35D).
27. We put on Christ when we were _ _ _ _ _ _ _ into Christ.
29. One's _ _ _ _ _ does not save them.
31. Even a covenant of _ _ _ cannot be invalidated.
33. The law served as our _ _ _ _ _ to bring us unto Christ.
34. Some of the faith in Galatia did not _ _ _ _ the truth.
35. The remainder of the statement in (24 Down) is 'in the _ _ _ _ _ of God.'
38. If we are of Christ, we _ _ _ _ _ _ Abraham's seed.
40. Before faith in Christ, we were kept _ _ _ _ _ the law.
42. There is neither _ _ _ _ _ _ nor free.
43. The scripture has concluded all to be under _ _ _ _ _ so that, (to 36A).
47. _ _ is the one.
48. The _ _ _ _ _ was given because of the transgressions of man.

Letter To Galatians-3, KJV

(Numbers read from left to right, line by line, whether clue is Across or Down. Blank spaces in a clue does not indicate the number of spaces in an answer.)

Letter To Galatians-4
Galatians 4, KJV

(Note: Numbers read from left to right, whether clue is Across of Down. Also, the number of blank spaces in a clue does not indicate number of spaces in an answer.)

Across Clues for Letter To Galatians-4:

2. Temptation is the same as a test or _ _ _ _ _ _.
4. "Ye have not _ _ _ _ _ me at all." (Paul said to Galatian church).
8. A guardian is said to be a _ _ _ _ _ _ _ in this chapter.
9. Mount Sinai is in _ _ _ _ _.
10. While an heir is a _ _ _ _ _, he . . . (to 19 Down).
11. Paul referred to the infirmity of his _ _ _ _ _ in verse fourteen.
14. The son of _ _ _ _ _ was born after the flesh.
16. The church at Galatia received Paul as an _ _ _ _ _ _ of God.
17. "_ _ little children . . ."
18. Paul reminded the Galatians that they would have given him their _ _ _ _ if it had been possible.
20. Christian believers are the children of _ _ _ _ _ _ _, as was Isaac.
21. God's Son was sent to _ _ _ _ _ _ those who were under the law; . . . (see 3D).
23. If we insist on trying to live under the law, we put ourselves in _ _ _ _ _ _.
25. Jesus was born subject to the _ _ _ _ _.
28. Those born after the flesh will _ _ _ _ _ _ those born according to the Spirit.
29. A governor's job is to _ _ _ _ _ _ _ _ or manage a minor's possessions.
33. (From 41 Down), ". . . the son of the _ _ _ _ woman shall not be heir with the son of the free woman."
34. When we were children, according to Paul, we were subject to the elements of the _ _ _ _ _ _.
35. Verse twelve says, "_ _ as I am;"
36. Paul compared his work with the Galatians to _ _ _ _ _ pains.
40. We are children of God by faith _ _ Christ Jesus.
42. Paul wrote that the births of Abraham sons were _ _ _ _ _ _.
46. 'God sent _ _ _ _ _ his Son . . .'
48. In verse fourteen, Paul recalled how the Galatian church did not despise him nor _ _ _ _ _ _ him.
49. The Jerusalem which is _ _ _ _ _ is free.
50. A governor is the same as a manager or _ _ _ _ _.
51. 'the fullness of _ _ _ _.'
52. Paul wrote, "for I am as ye _ _ _."
53. We are _ _ more servants in bondage under the law.

Down:

1. This puzzle content created by _ _ johnson, (03.23.2005).
2. Paul feared becoming an enemy because he told the _ _ _ _ _ _.
3. (From 21A) . . . so that we might be _ _ _ _ _ _ _ as his sons.

(Down Clues Continued On Following Page)

Galatians-4 Down Clues Continued:

5. To be 'made' means to come into _ _ _ _ _ _, be born, or come to pass.
6. Abba, in verse six, is Aramaic for _ _ _ _ _.
7. He is our father.
10. Paul writes that Hagar is in bondage with her _ _ _ _ _ _.
11. Sarah was the _ _ _ _ woman in verse twenty-three.
12. Because we are sons of God, the Spirit of his Son is in our _ _ _ _ _ .
13. _ _ _ _ _ _ _ was born to a servant woman.
15. An _ _ _ _ _ _ _ _ is the same as a symbol.
17. The Jerusalem above is said to be the _ _ _ _ _ _ of us all.
19. (Con't from 10 Across) . . . is said to be the same as a _ _ _ _ _ _.
22. _ _ _ _ _ _ was born to a free woman.
24. Sarah's son was born _ _ _ _ _ _ to the promise.
26. Paul wrote that he was _ _ _ _ _ _ for the Galatians.
27. Believers of faith in Jesus are made _ _ _ _ of God through Christ.
30. 'Abba Father' is an affectionate term of _ _ _ _ _ _ _ _.
31. The births of Isaac and Ishmael were compared to two _ _ _ _ _ _.
32. Hagar is said to correspond to the earthly _ _ _ _ _ _.
37. ". . . The desolate hath many more children than she which hath a _ _ _ _ _."
38. When we believe in Jesus, God gives us the _ _ _ _ _ _ of his Son.
39. We are known _ _ God.
41. She told her husband to 'Cast out the bondwoman and her son', (to 33 Across).
43. 'Lord' in verse one really means _ _ _ _ _ .
44. Abraham had more than _ _ _ son.
45. Hagar was a symbol of Mount _ _ _ _ _.
47. Jesus was born of a _ _ _ _ _ _.
50. Verse seven points out that a believer is no longer a servant, but a _ _ _ _ _.

Galatians-5

1) Stand fast therefore in the liberty wherewith Christ hath made us free, and be not entangled again with the yoke of bondage.
2) Behold, I Paul say unto you, that if ye be circumcised, Christ shall profit you nothing.
3) For I testify again to every man that is circumcised, that he is a debtor to do the whole law.
4) Christ is become of no effect unto you, whosoever of you are justified by the law; ye are fallen from grace.
5) For we through the Spirit wait for the hope of righteousness by faith.
6) For in Jesus Christ neither circumcision availeth any thing, nor uncircumcision; but faith which worketh by love.
7) Ye did run well; who did hinder you that ye should not obey the truth?
8) This persuasion [cometh] not of him that calleth you.
9) A little leaven leaveneth the whole lump.
10) I have confidence in you through the Lord, that ye will be none otherwise minded: but he that troubleth you shall bear his judgment, whosoever he be.
11) And I, brethren, if I yet preach circumcision, why do I yet suffer persecution? then is the offence of the cross ceased.
12) I would they were even cut off which trouble you.
13) For, brethren, ye have been called unto liberty; only [use] not liberty for an occasion to the flesh, but by love serve one another.
14) For all the law is fulfilled in one word, [even] in this; Thou shalt love thy neighbour as thyself.
15) But if ye bite and devour one another, take heed that ye be not consumed one of another.
16) [This] I say then, Walk in the Spirit, and ye shall not fulfill the lust of the flesh.
17) For the flesh lusteth against the Spirit, and the Spirit against the flesh: and these are contrary the one to the other: so that ye cannot do the things that ye would.
18) But if ye be led of the Spirit, ye are not under the law.
19) Now the works of the flesh are manifest, which are [these]; Adultery, fornication, uncleanness, lasciviousness,
20) Idolatry, witchcraft, hatred, variance, emulations, wrath, strife, seditions, heresies,
21) Envyings, murders, drunkenness, revellings, and such like: of the which I tell you before, as I have also told [you] in time past, that they which do such things shall not inherit the kingdom of God.
22) But the fruit of the Spirit is love, joy, peace, longsuffering, gentleness, goodness, faith,
23) Meekness, temperance: against such there is no law.
24) And they that are Christ's have crucified the flesh with the affections and lusts.
25) If we live in the Spirit, let us also walk in the Spirit.
26) Let us not be desirous of vain glory, provoking one another, envying one another.

Letter To Galatians-5
Galatians 5, KJV

(Numbers read from left to right, line by line, whether clue is Across or Down. Number of spaces in a clue does not indicate the number of spaces in an answer.)

Across:

1. "Behold, I _ _ _ _ say unto you . . ."
3. 'Christ has made us _ _ _ _.'
5. ". . . if I yet preach circumcision, why do I yet _ _ _ _ _ _ . . . ?"
9. 'The _ _ _ _ _ of the Spirit is love, joy, . . .'
10. To _ _ _ _ by faith means that the law is of no consequence for us.
12. "For the _ _ _ _ _ lusteth against the Spirit . . ."
15. (From 46 Down) " . . . and _ _ shall not fulfill the lust of the flesh."
16. We are urged to be _ _ _ _ suffering.
17. Take heed not to _ _ _ _ and devour one another.
19. 'Stand fast in the _ _ _ _ _ that Christ has given us.'
21. Being circumcised does _ _ _ guarantee salvation.
23. Anyone attempting to be justified by the law are fallen from _ _ _ _ _.
24. There is _ _ law against meekness and temperance, nor any other fruit of the Spirit.
25. 'Who hindered you that you should not _ _ _ _ the truth?' (Also Gal 3:1).

Across Clues Continued for Galatians-5:

29. _ _ _ I know Him.
30. Waiting in verse five is done by _ _ _ _ _.
32. Circumcision was of the _ _ _ for the Jews.
35. "For, brethren, ye have been _ _ _ _ _ _ unto liberty; . . ."
37. _ _ _ _ _ and faith are fruits of the Spirit.
40. Envy and _ _ _ _ _ _ are works of the flesh.
43. _ _ _ _ _ _ is considered a work of the flesh.
44. The Son of God is _ _ _ _ _. (2 wds).
46. "Now the _ _ _ _ _ of the flesh are manifest," (Verse 19).
48. 'All the law is fulfilled in _ _ _ word . . .'
49. Leaven is a metaphor for _ _ _ _ _ doctrine in these passages.
50. 'Be _ _ _ of the Spirit.'
51. Verse one warns us not to be entangled in the _ _ _ _ of bondage.

Down:

2. Serve one another with _ _ _ _ _.
4. If you try to live by the law, Christ is become of no _ _ _ _ _ _ upon you.
5. 'For we through the _ _ _ _ _ wait for the hope of righteousness . . .'
6. Manifest means apparent or _ _ _ _ _ _ _.
7. Temperance is the same as _ _ _ _ control.
8. If one insists on keeping part of the law, they would be required to keep the _ _ _ _ _ law.
11. People who indulge in fleshly works will not _ _ _ _ _ _ _ the kingdom of God.
13. 'A little _ _ _ _ _ leaveneth the whole lump.'
14. Paul wrote that the circumcised were in _ _ _ _ to the whole law.
18. Christians must not _ _ _ _ one another.
20. 'Ye did _ _ _ well . . . ;'
22. Love thy neighbor as _ _ _ _ _.
26. ". . . he that troubleth you shall _ _ _ _ his judgment . . ."
27. '. . . we wait for the _ _ _ _ of righteousness.'
28. We should _ _ _ _ in the Spirit.
31. There _ _ _ multiple fruits of the Spirit.
33. Vain glory translates as _ _ _ _ _ in verse 26.
34. Faith works_ _ love.
35. We who are of Christ have _ _ _ _ _ _ _ _ _ the flesh . . .
36. _ _ you know Him?
38. 'I wish they would _ _ _ themselves off from you . . .'
39. You are not _ _ _ _ _ the law, if you are led by the Spirit.
41. This work of the flesh involves sexual unfaithfulness to your spouse.
42. ". . . take _ _ _ _ that ye be not consumed one of another."
43. "I _ _ _ _ confidence in you . . ."
45. This puzzle content created by _ _ johnson, (03.25.2005).
46. "_ _ _ _ in the Spirit . . ." (con't in 15 Across)
47. Jesus is the _ _ _ of God.

61

Letter to Galatians 6
Galatians 6, KJV

(Note: Numbers read from left to right, line by line, whether clue is Across or Down. Number of spaces in clue does not indicate number of letters in answer.)

Letter to Galatians 6, KJV

Across Clues:

3. (Con't from 6D) ". . . that they may _ _ _ _ _ in your flesh."
5. To bear your own 'burden' in verse five is a _ _ _ _ _ _ _ _ responsibility.
8. For in Christ Jesus, circumcision or not, does not avail you _ _ _ thing, (v 15).
9. There were problems in the early church just as there are _ _ _ _ _.
10. The designation of the Galatian letter was to the _ _ _ _ _ _ there.
13. (From 43D) . . . 'especially to those who are of the household of _ _ _ _ _, (v 10).
14. To _ _ is a state of being.
15. To prove means to _ _ _ _ _. (v 4)
16. There are _ _ _ chapters of Galatians.
18. Every _ _ _ shall be responsible for himself, (v 5).
19. What you _ _ _ _ proves what you have sowed.
20. Christians are to _ _ _ _ one another up in love.
21. Being transformed into a _ _ _ creature benefits us spiritually.
23. Paul wrote that it did not matter whether one was circumcised or _ _ _ _ _.
25. An epistle is a _ _ _ _ _.
26. We are told to bear one another's _ _ _ _ _ _ _, even as we bear our own, (to 41A).
27. He was blinded for three days.
28. If one _ _ _ _ to the flesh, (to 34D).
30. Being overtaken translates to being found out or _ _ _ _ _. (v1)
33. No human being is _ _ _ _ _.
37. Another word for letter is _ _ _ _ _.
38. This puzzle content designed by _ _ _ _ Johnson, (March 2005).
41. (From 26A), '. . . and so fulfill the law of _ _ _ _ _.'
42. Jesus is _ _ _ _.
44. Communicating in verse six means _ _ _ _ _ _ _ what you know with others.
45. To make a 'fair show in the flesh' translates to 'make a _ _ _ _ showing,' (v 12)
48. (From 24D) . . . , '. . . and mercy upon the _ _ _ _ _ _ of God,' (v 16).
49. Do not let yourself be _ _ _ _ _ _ _, (v 7).
51. (From 46D) "save in the _ _ _ _ _ of our Lord Jesus Christ, . . ."
54. We are to _ _ _ _ _ _ _ one another in the spirit of meekness, (to 62A).
55. As a man thinks in his heart, so he _ _ _. (Proverbs 23:7).
56. We will all reap our reward in _ _ _ season.
57. 'Save' in verse fourteen refers to _ _ _ _ _.
60. A 2-letter word that indicates a condition to a statement _ _ _ _ _.

(Clues Continued Next Page)

Galatians-6 Across Clues Continued:

61. Let him that is taught in the _ _ _ _ communicate to others.
62. (From 54A) . . . , and consider ourselves, _ _ _ _ we also be tempted.' (v 1)
64. To be meek, means to be _ _ _ _ _.
65. _ _ _ _ _ met Paul on the Damascus road.

Down:

1. Creature in verse 15 alludes to _ _ _ _ _.
2. Be _ _ _ _ in doing well, (2 wds).
3. The writer begins and ends his letters with a word about _ _ _ _ _.
4. (From 16D) . . . , 'he shall reap _ _ _ _ everlasting of the Spirit.' (v 8)
6. Those who are circumcised do not themselves keep the _ _ _, (v 13).
7. God is not, and will not be _ _ _ _.
11. Paul wrote this letter with his own _ _ _ _ _.
12. 'Faint not' in verse nine translates to 'do not lose _ _ _ _ _.'
16. 'But if one sows to the _ _ _ _ _ _ . . .' (con't in 4D)
17. To _ _ _ _ _ _ _ _ _ in verse 12 refers to 'compel'.
22. Those who are Spiritual refers to those who _ _ _ _ in the Spirit.
23. Galatians is in the _ _ _ Testament.
24. '_ _ _ _ _ be unto those that walk according to this rule, . . .' (con't in 48A).
27. '. . . let every man _ _ _ _ _ his own work.'
28. Rejoice in your own _ _ _ _.
29. Brethren translates to _ _ _ _ _ in Christ.
31. A 3-letter word that indicates doubt or change of circumstances.
32. Paul was an apostle to the _ _ _ _ _, (Gal 2:7).
34. (From 28A) . . . , one will reap _ _ _ _ _ _.
35. (From 58D) 'he _ _ _ _ _ _ _ _ himself.'
36. Some of Paul's letters were written while he was in _ _ _ _ _.
39. Peter was apostle to the _ _ _ _ _, (Gal 2:7).
40. The Greek translation of 'burdens' in verse two refers to _ _ _ _ _ _ weaknesses.
43. Do _ _ _ _ unto all men . . . , (to 13A).
46. "But _ _ _ forbid that I should glory . . ." (to 51A).
47. Those of the circumcision _ _ _ _ _ _ to have you circumcised . . ." (to 3A).
50. Paul said, "the world is _ _ _ _ _ _ _ _ _ unto me." (v 14)
52. (From 59D) . . . , We who are spiritual must _ _ _ _ _ _ _ those who have slipped.
53. Before he was called Paul, he was _ _ _ _ _.
58. If one _ _ _ _ _ _ he is something, when he is nothing . . . , (to 35D).
59. If our brothers/sisters are found in a _ _ _ _ _, (v1), (to 52D).
63. The initials of this puzzle's creator is _ _ _ _.

**Luke's Genealogy of Jesus,
Luke 1:1-4, 3:23-38, KJV**

(Puzzle Grid on Page 67)

Clues Across:

1. His name is mentioned several times throughout Luke's record of Jesus' lineage.
3. The beginning word for verse 23 of Luke 3.
9. Salah or Sala in verse 35 refers to _ _ _ _ _ _.
10. Luke was a companion of _ _ _ _ in the latter days of his life, (2 Tim 4:11).
11. _ _ _ _ was also a companion of Paul, (2 Tim 4:11).
15. A declaration can also be called a _ _ _ _ _ _ _ _ _.
16. Neri was the _ _ _ _ _ father of Zorobabel or Zerubbabel, (v27).
20. Jesus began his ministry when he was about how old.
21. Son of David to advance lineage to Jesus. (Lu 3:31; 2 Sam 5:13-16).
22. The father of the tribe of Israel who carried forth the line of birth to Jesus?
24. David had _ _ _ _ _ brothers, (1 Sam 16:10-13).
26. The written progression of one's forefathers is referred to as their _ _ _ _ _ _ _ _ _.
28. These words have been added for clarity in every verse from Luke 3:23-38, (2 wds).
30. There are many _ _ _ _ _ _ in Luke's record of Jesus that Matthew did not mention.
32. A son of Noah who carried lineage to Jesus, (v36).
33. A son of Eber, (v35).
35. The wife of Boaz was not of Israel but was from _ _ _ _.
36. The father of Abraham.
37. Another word continually used in these passages.
40. A narrative is simply the telling of a _ _ _ _ _.
41. Matthew lists Joseph as the son of Jacob; Luke lists Joseph as the son of _ _ _ _, (v23).
42. _ _ _ _ is not mentioned in Luke's genealogy, (hint: birth mother).
43. Noah's father was _ _ _ _ _ _.
44. Luke lists Jesus' genealogy before Abraham, or Adam; he traces it back to _ _ _ _ _.
45. Matthew and Luke agree that Zerubbabel was the _ _ _ _ of Salathiel.
46. The first son of God according to Luke?
47. David's father.

(Down Clues Next Page):

65

Luke's Genealogy Continued:
Down:

1. Puzzle content designed by tj _ _ _ _ _ _ _, (12.12.04).
2. Sometimes, the immediate father of one is not listed, but rather a _____.
4. A son of Lamech.
5. Luke's narrative was _ _ _ _ _ _ _ _ _ upon those with firsthand knowledge, (Lu 1:1-2).
6. Ragau in verse 35 is the same as _ _ _.
7. Theophilus was referred to as 'most _ _ _ _ _ _ _ _.'
8. Luke is said to have been a _____, (Col 4:14)
12. Once the list of forefathers get to _ _ _ _ _ (v31), the lineage matches Matthew's through Abraham.
13. The wife of Boaz was considered a _ _ _ _ _ _ _.
14. _ _ _ _ _ people wrote of the good news that was being spread throughout the countryside, (Lu 1:1).
17. It appears that three generations are _ _ _ _ _ _ _ _ in the genealogy given in Matthew.
18. The beginning word for verses 24-38 of Luke 3, is _ _ _ _ _.
19. He declared that it seemed good for him to write what he knew.
23. The man who married Ruth was _ _ _ _, (Ruth 4:13).
25. Luke was a _ _ _ _ _ _ _ at one time to the author of the epistle to the Colossians.
27. You could say that Luke was an _ _ _ witness.
29. _ _ _ _ _ was the legal son of Joseph.
31. Methuselah and his father _ _ _ _ _ are in the genealogy of Jesus.
32. One translation for Jesus is 'Jehovah is _ _ _ _ _ _ _ _ _,' or Savior.[1,2]
34. Luke said he had a _ _ _ _ _ _ _ understanding of all things from above.
38. Luke writes that Jesus was the _____ son of Joseph.
39. Luke's writing is to one called Theophilus, better translated as _ _ _ _ _ _ of God.[3]
43. Who penned the book of Luke?

Luke's Genealogy of Jesus,
Luke 1:1-4, 3:23-38, KJV

(Note: Numbers read from left to right, line by line, whether clue is Across or Down)

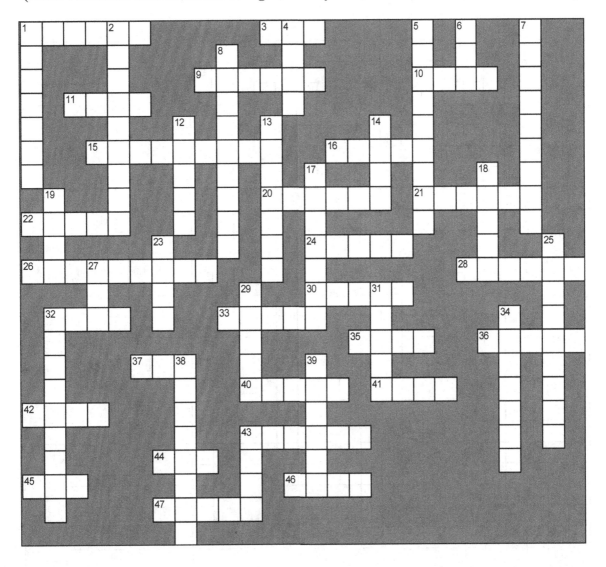

Chapter & Verse

Mary, *Elisabeth, and Birth of John the Baptist
Luke 1:39-80, KJV

(Note: Numbers read from left to right, line by line, whether clue is Across or Down)

*Elizabeth used instead of Elisabeth in the puzzle spelling

68

Clues for Mary, *Elizabeth, and John:
*(Note spelling for Elizabeth previous page):

Across:

5. As soon as Zechariah wrote down the name of his son, his _____ was opened.
7. John was to be called the prophet of the _____, according to his prophet father.
8. Jewish sons are _____ on the day of their circumcision.
10. _____ is called God's servant, (hint: a people).
12. The name of God is deemed to be _____.
13. Zechariah prophesied . . . , "To perform the mercy _____ to our fathers . . .", (to 19D).
15. The translation of fear in verse 74 refers to serving God _____.
20. When Elizabeth heard the greeting of her relative, her unborn _____ leaped for joy in her womb.
23. Opposite of in.
24. Mary declared that her spirit rejoiced in God her _____.
25. To magnify is to _____.
27. The words 'day-spring' in verse 78 figuratively refers to the coming of the _____.
28. Mary became pregnant when the _____ overshadowed her, (2 wds).
30. Jesus is _____ whom Isaiah spoke of in Isaiah 9:6.
32. The father of Jesus is ____.
34. When Zechariah could speak again, he immediately praised _____.
35. Mary visited with Elizabeth for _____ months.
37. The _____ were referred to as holy in this passage.
42. Mary said, 'My soul doth _____ the Lord.'
43. A word that gives one a choice.
44. Blessed is she who _____, (v 45), (to 38D).
45. This puzzle content created by tj _____, (12.11.2004).
47. A state of being.
50. Referring to his son, Zechariah wrote, 'His name is _____.'
51. Elizabeth said to Mary," _____ art thou among women."
52. Israel spoke of _____ as their father.
53. A simple conjunction that connects ideas, and/or phrases.
54. Mary knew something about the Lord as she praised his works: "He put down the _____ from their thrones."
55. (From 56 Across), '. . . and to give _____ of salvation unto his people.'
56. John would go before the face of the Lord to _____ the way, (back to 55A).

(Down Clues Next Page):

Mary, Elizabeth, and John Continued:
Down:

1. Even before Mary mentioned her condition, Elizabeth said, ". . . blessed is the _____ of thy womb."
2. As Elizabeth's baby leaped within her, she was _____ with the Holy Ghost.
3. John spent much of his time in the _____.
4. Israel is delivered from their enemies so that they might serve God without _____.
6. Zechariah was filled with the _____ and prophesied, (2 wds).
9. Both Mary and Elizabeth learned of their sons impending births from an _____.
11. Knowledge of salvation gives _____ to those that sit in darkness.
14. Mary entered _____ the house of Zechariah and saluted Elizabeth.
15. The son of Elizabeth and Zechariah was John the _____, (Luke 9:19).
16. Elizabeth's relatives and neighbors wanted to name her son after his _____.
17. Salutation is the same as a _____.
18. _____ will be saved from all their enemies.
19. (From 13 Across) . . . "and to remember his holy _____."
21. All generations will call Mary _____.
22. The Holy Ghost is the _____ as the Holy Spirit.
26. (From 28D), and went into the _____ country to visit Elizabeth.
28. Mary left her home town in _____, (to 26D).
29. Zechariah prophesied saying, ". . . Blessed be the Lord God of Israel, for he has visited and _____ his people."
31. John's father was _____.
33. Zechariah wrote his son's name on a tablet because he could not _____.
36. Zechariah also prophesied that God had, 'raised up a _____ of salvation.'
38. (From 44 Across) ". . . for there shall be a _____ of those things which were told her from the Lord."
39. Performance is the same as the _____ of a promise.
40. The author of Luke.
41. Elizabeth wanted to know, "why the mother of _____ should come to me" (2 wds).
46. Jewish sons are circumcised on the _____ day of their life, (Lev 12:3).
48. God has _____ on those that fear him.
49. To _____ Him is to revere him by showing awesome respect for Him.
50. Elizabeth lived in a city of _____.
54. _____ was chosen by God to give birth to Jesus, the savior of the world.

About Moses

Moses was born during a time when all Hebrew baby boys
were under a death sentence. Because of this edict
passed down by a new Pharaoh of Egypt,
The mother of Moses sought to hide her son.

You see, this Pharaoh was very insecure
and feared that the children of Israel would one day
out number the Egyptians, and perhaps join forces
With Egypt's enemies—in case of war.

The King even tried to afflict the Israelites with
harsh working conditions, but the severe labor
and living situation served only to make
The people of Israel produce more children.

So the king decided to have all the boy babies killed.
Moses' mother hid him from the soldiers
in a little home-made floating raft
and pushed him down the river.
His big sister watched to see
What would happen to her baby brother.

The king's sister found Moses
and kept him to become her own son.
He was raised as an Egyptian,
in the courts of the very Pharaoh
Who had ordered him to be killed.

And so is the story of the child Moses.

Moses, Exodus 1-4, Genesis 25, KJV

(Numbers read from left to right, line by line, whether clue is Across or Down)

Across:

1. Moses being a _____ child means he was pleasant, well pleasing to God, (Ex 2:2).
4. Jethro was the _____ of Midian.
7. The mountain of God was said to be in the _____ of the desert, (2 wds; Ex 3:1).
11. Moses' wife had _____ sisters.
12. (From 46D) because the place where Moses stood was _____ ground.
16. Can be cattle, sheep or goats.
17. Moses' sister, (Num 26:59).
18. Because of his fear, Moses hid his _____ from God.
19. Moses' father, (Ex 6:20).
21. The Lord described himself to Moses in two words: _____.
23. Moses' father married his father's _____.
24. The mountain of God.
25. The Pharaoh's daughter gave Moses his _____, (Ex 2:10).
28. Smite, smote, hit repeatedly.
31. Moses met God while tending his father-in-law's _____.
32. Gershom translates as stranger or _____.

Moses Across Clues continued:

33. LORD, all caps interprets as _____.
35. Killed.
37. Moses' brother.
38. Eliezer is translated as 'My God is _____', (Ex 18:3-4).
40. Moses was of the _____ tribe.
41. The bush burned with fire, but was not _____, (Ex 3:2).
43. Flags in Ex 2:3 are really _____.
45. Strive, contend, or quarrel.
48. God promised Israel a land of milk and _____.
49. God of Abraham, and of Isaac, and of _____.
50. Moses' mother.
51. God became angry when Moses _____ God, Ex 4:14).
52. The LORD told Moses that he had surely seen the _____ of Israel in Egypt.

Down:

1. Moses' first son, (Ex 2;22).
2. Hebrew for Jehovah is _____.
3. _____ was a son of Abraham and Keturah, (Gen 25:1-2).
5. Puzzle content designed by _____, (12.08.2007).
6. The angel of the LORD appeared to Moses in the _____ of a burning bush.
8. The land of Moses' wife's family was named after a descendant of _____.
9. _____ is called God's first-born son, (Ex 4:22).
10. God commissioned Moses to lead Israel out of _____.
13. Moses was _____ years old when he reclaimed his alliance to Israel, (Acts 7:23).
14. Moses' wife. (Ex 2:21).
15. God hardened Pharaoh's heart _____ times, (Ex 7 - 11).
20. Pharaoh's daughter knew right away that the baby Moses was a _____, (Ex 2:6).
22. His name means 'drawn out', (Ex 2;10).
23. When Moses intervened, Israel was told to make bricks without _____, (Ex5:1-7).
25. The river in this setting is mostly referred to as 'the river', (Ex 4:9).
26. God referred to Israel as 'my _____.'
27. Pharaoh's daughter found Moses floating in a roughly made _____, (Ex 2:3).
29. Moses' second son, (Ex 18:4).
30. Moses told the LORD that he had a slow _____, (Ex 4:10).
32. Moses killed an Egyptian and hid him in the _____.
34. 'The face of Pharaoh' refers to the _____ of Pharaoh, (Ex 2:15).
36. Abraham sent his sons by Keturah to live in the _____ country, (Ex 25:6).
37. Moses' mother was also his great _____.
39. Reuel translates as _____, (Ex 2:18).
41. The promised land.
42. The Egyptians made Israel's lives _____ with hard bondage, Ex 1:14).
44. Same mountain as Mt. Horeb, (Ex 3:1-17; Ex 19).
46. _____ told Moses to remove his shoes, (to 12A).
47. Moses returned to Egypt with his wife and his _____, (Ex 4:19).

Moses Glimpses The Land
Numbers 20:2-13; Deuteronomy 3:24-29, KJV

Across:

4. This special land was first made known to ____. (Gen 15:7, 18).
7. Moses ____ the rock twice instead of doing as the LORD had said, (Num 2: 8-11).
9. This good land was known as the ____ land.
13. He lead the children of Israel after Moses died.
14. Moses observed the new land from atop Mount _____.
16. Numbers is considered a book of the ____.
17. When Israel rebelled against Moses and Aaron, they also rebelled against the ____.
18. Moses said the land across the Jordan was ____ land.
23. Moses, nor Aaron, crossed over the _____, (to 27A).
27. (From 23A) . . . , and subsequently, _____ entered into the new land.
29. Aaron died at Mount ____, (Num 20:28).
30. Meribah translates as ____.
32. The story of God's anger at Moses is told in Deuteronomy and in ____.
34. Moses and Aaron fell on their ____ to pray because of the anger of the people, (pl).
36. The LORD told Moses to ____ to the rock.
38. Mighty.
41. There was water enough for the ____ also, (Num 11).
42. Puzzle designed by tj _____, (12.08.07).
43. The people were afraid they would ____ in the desert.
44. The people called the land they traveled an _____ land, (Num 20:5).

Down:

1. Moses _____ the greatness of the LORD, (Deu3:24).
2. The valley against Beth-peor was in the land of the ____.
3. Angry is written as _____ in Deuteronomy 3:26 of King James Bible.
5. God's hand is ____.
6. God was displeased with Moses and Aaron for they failed to sanctify him before _____.
8. The people voiced thoughts of having stayed in _____.
10. Pisgah was located in the territory of _____.
11. He took over the office of Priest after Aaron, (Num 20:26).
12. Chode or _____.
15. The _____ of the LORD appeared unto them.
19. Moses' name translates as _____.
20. His name translates as 'Jehovah is salvation.'
21. Moses accused Israel as being _____.
22. 'Beyond Jordan' means the _____ side of the river.
23. The one true God.

Moses Glimpses The Land, Down Clues Continued:

24. Israel turned against Moses because they did not have any ____.
25. The first High Priest.
26. Aaron was Moses' _____.
28. God advised Moses to _____ no more about the matter.
31. 'This side Jordan' refers to ____ of the river.
33. The books that Moses penned are referred to as the 'law of _____.'
35. Moses _____ that God would allow him to go into the new land.
36. Eleazar was the _____ of Aaron.
37. Sanctify.
39. God made water spring forth from a _____.
40. LORD (all caps) represents the proper name of _____.

Moses Glimpses The Land

(Note: Numbers read from left to right, whether clue is Across or Down)

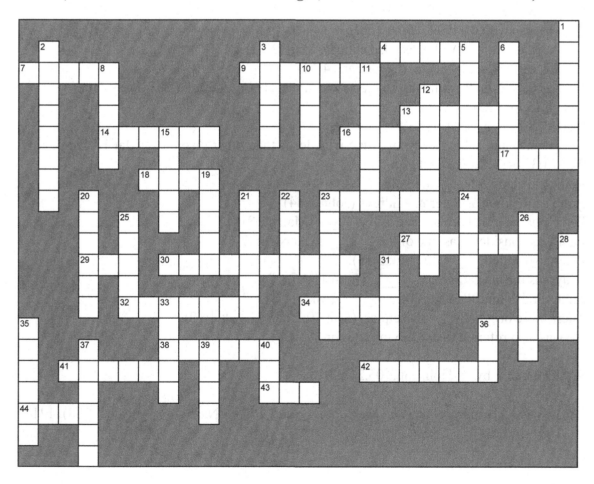

Mostly Disciples,
Various New Testament Scripture, KJV

Clues:

Deeds or _____

This James (the less), the son of _____, (Matthew (Mat.) 10:3)

He helped ease trepidation about Paul, (Acts 9:26-27)

Bart who? (Mat 10:3)

Not Simon Peter, but Simon the _____, (Mat 10:4)

NT translated as new _____, (Hebrew (Heb) 8:6-7)

Saul was blinded on his way to_____, (Acts 1:1-9)

Two sets of brothers were _____, by trade, (Mat 4:18; Luke 5:10; Mark 1:29)

There are four NT _____

NT translates in this language

OT translates in this language

The NT is written about _____ (Heb 12:24)

James and _____ of Zebedee were brothers, (Mark 10:35)

He betrayed Jesus, (Mat 26:14-16; 25)

He was also called a thief, (John 12:6)

Matthew, the son of Alphaeus, also called, (Mark 2:14)

He was called the physician, (Colossians 4:14)

He was helpful in the ministry to the new churches being started, (2 Timothy 4:11)

Tax collector, (Mark 2:14)

Saul also known as, (Acts 13:9)

____ James and John spent more time with Jesus than other disciples, (Mat 17:1; Mk 5:37, 9:2, 13:3; 14:33; Luke 8:51)

Mark traveled with ___ and Paul

From same town as Peter & Andrew, (John 1:44)

Peter's name translates as 'petros' or _____,(Mat. 4:18). [1]

Paul was considered as one of the _____ in Acts 16:37-38

Peter also called _____, (Mark 3:16)

Didymus means double or _____, (John 11:16), [2]

James and John called sons of _____, (Mk 3:17)

There were originally ___ Disciples, (Mat 10:2; 20:17; Mk 4:10)

He was also referred to as Didymus, (John 11:16)

Puzzle content by ___ johnson, (05.31.08)

[1,2] Wayne A. Brindle, et al., *The King James Study Bible*. (Nashville: Nelson, 1988), 1414, 1631-1632

Mostly Disciples
Various Scripture, KJV

Figure out what words the clues on the previous page represent. Then circle the words in the grid. Words can go across, down and in three diagonals. You may also find words not described in the clues.

```
M  T  Q  L  M  T  J  L  L  Q  M  K  J  O  H  N  H  R  B  P
N  H  U  L  H  L  U  K  T  J  L  D  A  M  A  S  C  U  S  M
W  K  R  O  L  L  D  F  T  M  E  P  R  K  L  N  L  R  J  N
E  L  M  E  K  T  A  V  R  M  Z  S  E  H  D  F  E  B  F  X
M  A  V  G  W  Z  S  L  F  H  K  T  U  T  I  T  M  G  D  Y
S  I  G  C  T  L  K  N  B  K  T  R  M  S  E  L  P  A  U  L
G  X  N  P  Q  V  C  M  N  P  S  B  H  P  B  R  D  W  V  T
Z  D  B  C  H  J  S  M  R  L  L  E  M  A  Z  X  M  L  A  P
G  M  V  K  L  I  S  I  E  J  R  H  R  W  B  L  A  B  L  L
J  U  D  A  S  W  L  P  M  M  Z  T  L  W  A  G  T  J  P  N
R  R  T  Q  E  N  S  I  E  O  H  L  D  M  R  J  T  M  H  T
A  F  V  R  X  O  L  N  P  O  N  P  V  E  N  K  H  D  A  R
B  C  B  T  G  M  K  J  L  N  N  K  E  C  A  L  E  G  E  C
T  E  T  L  W  Q  T  O  Q  Y  R  K  W  G  B  P  W  D  U  K
H  Z  K  S  L  E  M  R  N  A  K  R  P  P  A  B  N  G  S  N
F  L  W  D  K  E  L  Z  M  Z  D  O  X  D  S  U  P  M  I  K
B  G  D  Q  W  N  Y  V  N  R  N  M  W  X  H  N  L  W  R  R
C  O  V  E  N  A  N  T  E  O  K  A  D  T  L  V  T  K  C  D
L  Y  N  N  V  Y  W  L  D  C  A  N  A  A  N  I  T  E  D  B
G  Q  V  P  T  W  L  N  X  K  P  S  J  K  W  D  L  T  R  H
```

Names Jesus Known By, Part I
Various Scriptures, KJV

Names Jesus Known By, Part I; Circle words in Puzzle Grid, page 79:

Alpha and Omega, (Rev 22:3)

Bread of Life, (John 6:35, 48)

Christ, (Matt 16:16, 20)

Head of the Church, (Ephesians 5:23; Colossians 1:18)

Immanuel, (Isaiah 7:14; 8:8)

Jesus, (Matthew 1:16, 18)

King of the Jews, (Matthew 2:2; 27:37)

Lamb of God, (John 1:29, 36)

Light of the World, (John 8:12)

Lion of Judah, (Hosea 5:14)

Lord, (Matthew 17:4; Acts 9:5; 10:36; Romans 6:23)

Master, (Mathew 12:38; 19:16; 23:8; John 13:13)

Messiah, (Dan 9:25, 26)

Prince of Peace, (Isaiah 9:6)

Rabbi, (John 1:49; 3:2)

Rock, (Psalm 18:2; 28:1; 62:2, 1Corinthians 10:4)

Savior, (also spelled Saviour), (Luke 2:11; John 4:42; 2Timothy 1:10)

Shepherd, Psalm 23:1; Matthew 2:6; Hebrew 13:29, John 10:2)

Shield, (Psalm 3:3)

Sword, (of the Spirit)(Ephesians 6:17)

Teacher, (John 3:2)

The Door, (John 10:9)

The Way, (John 14:6)

True Vine, (John 15:1)

TJ Johnson (Puzzle designer, 12.04.05)

Word, (John 1:1)

Names Jesus Known By, Part I
Various Scriptures, KJV

Find and circle the words (may be multiple words) listed on page 78. Words can go across from left to right, top to bottom, in three diagonals from left to right, up or down. You may also find unscripted words in the puzzle grid.

```
K  I  N  G  O  F  T  H  E  J  E  W  S  X  L  V  I  Y  T
R  L  Y  L  D  Z  X  Y  T  J  T  J  T  N  L  M  M  R  R
L  V  R  K  M  T  W  J  T  D  K  L  Z  D  M  R  L  K  J
L  N  T  H  B  D  J  Y  R  Y  I  F  R  A  A  Z  I  P  N
F  S  A  V  I  O  R  O  Q  O  N  E  N  G  R  L  G  R  H
L  V  T  R  H  V  W  V  N  K  H  U  E  A  T  S  H  I  E
K  M  L  N  R  B  P  O  C  C  E  M  B  K  R  H  T  N  A
D  T  S  A  R  R  F  O  A  L  O  B  J  R  U  E  O  C  D
M  O  H  H  M  J  R  E  C  D  I  Z  L  R  E  P  F  E  O
N  E  R  E  U  B  T  R  N  H  S  N  P  N  V  H  T  O  F
S  P  S  D  W  R  O  A  D  W  R  S  N  K  I  E  H  F  T
T  H  A  S  V  A  A  F  O  K  U  I  Z  T  N  R  E  P  H
C  H  I  D  I  H  Y  R  G  S  M  Q  S  N  E  D  W  E  E
F  Z  R  E  P  A  D  N  E  O  K  P  M  T  T  T  O  A  C
N  O  L  L  L  J  H  J  T  T  D  R  R  B  J  H  R  C  H
L  G  A  C  Z  D  Y  T  B  M  A  S  T  E  R  T  L  E  U
D  R  F  B  R  E  A  D  O  F  L  I  F  E  G  R  D  Z  R
M  N  Z  F  Z  Q  F  P  K  M  N  Q  Q  D  Z  M  N  K  C
J  Z  M  Z  R  H  L  N  N  G  T  H  E  D  O  O  R  N  H
```

Chapter & Verse

Names Jesus is Known By, Part II
Various Scripture, KJV

Find and circle the words listed on page following page. Words can go across and down, and in three diagonals from left to right, up or down; right to left. You may also find unscripted words in the puzzle grid.

```
E V E R L A S T I N G F A T H E R J H L D K
W O N D E R F U L H P I M M A N U E L V M T
N F A I T H F U L W I T N E S S J F H J H T
H V B F N Z V M P K B R J C Z D M T Y O K H
Y T I P M Q Q K W Q X E A N O P U X L N B E
B H S R E N M P W L N G L G Z R L I Q D C F
T E H G S B N R C X E L Y O T N H W Z B Y I
Q W O T S N S V N M M T C E V S R H Z E B R
R A P B I K V O O X H N H J X E F R L T R S
F Y K G A L T D N G Q T F T B R D L P R I T
Q Y C M H J N G I O B R A N C H A S O L D B
T X L M Z A S M O B F P M D L V T L O H E O
G J Z R A G E O W O G D L R E W L Z K N G R
Z L J H M H J N N N D J A H K E C J L J R N
R Q P O T R Z T Y O J S T V S L J B Z B O W
B L J H H N R D Z F F F H N I T O N M N O M
A L D Z N N C B W T O G U E K D H G C L M H
M R T K D Y S R R Y J O O D P L N E O M L P
G V K M G F Q O L L C W H D P H L R L S G P
J B C Y N F T I N P P N R W I T E X G I L Z
V G D K Z H L K M N D N R X A H N R L G F F
T S T E M O F J E S S E V B M M M L D C Y E
```

80

Names Jesus Is Known By, Part II
Find and circle following words or phrases in the grid on previous page:

Alpha and Omega, (Revelation, (Rev) 1:8)

Beloved Son, (Mark (Mk) 3:17; 2Peter (Pet) 1:17

Bishop, (1Pet 5:4)

Branch, (Isaiah (Is) 4:2; 11:1)

Bridegroom, (Matthew (Mat) 25:10)

Counsellor, (Is 9:6; notice spelling)

Everlasting Father, (Is 9:6)

Faithful Witness, (Rev 1:5)

Good Shepherd, (John 10:11, 14)

I AM, (Gen 15:7; Exodus (Ex) 3:14; Jo 8:58)

Immanuel, (Is 7:14; 8:8)

Lily of the Valley, (Song of Solomon (Sgs.) 2:1)

Logos, (John 1:1—Greek translation for Word)

Messiah, (Daniel (Dan) 9:25, 26)

Shiloh, (Gen 49:10)

Son of David, (Mat 9:27; 12:23; 22:44)

Son of God, (Mat 14:33; Mk 1:1; John 3:18)

Stem of Jesse, (Is 11:1)

The Firstborn, (Colossians 1:15)

The Life, (John 11:25)

The Mighty God, (Is 9:6)

The Truth, (John 14:6)

The Way, (John 14:6)

TJ Johnson, (designed this puzzle on 12.04.05)

Wonderful, (Is 9:6)

Names Jesus Known By, Part III
Find and circle names in grid, following page.

Angel of the Lord, (Gen 16:7-11; 1Chronicles 21:16)

Bright and Morning Star, (Rev 22:16)

Carpenter, (Mark 6:13)

First Fruit of the Dead, (Rev 1:5)

High Priest, (Hebrews 3:1)

Jesus Christ, (John1:17)

Jesus, (Mat 1:21)

Lamb, (Rev 5:12, 13))

Lamb without Blemish (1Peter 1:19)

Lord Jesus, (Acts 1:21; Acts 15:11; Luke 24:3)

Mary's Baby, (Mk 6:3; Luke 2:16, Christmas song)

Prince of Peace, (Is 9:6)

Prophet, (John 7:40; 9:7)

Root of David, (Rev 22:16)

Rose of Sharon, (Song of Solomon 2:1)

Seed of the Woman, (Gen 3:15)

Son of Man, (Dan 7:13; Mat 12:8; 16:13)

The Beginning, (Rev 22:13)

The Door, (John 10:7, 9)

The Ending, (Rev 1:8)

The First, (Rev 22:13)

The Last, (Rev 22:13)

The Lord, (Luke 2:1; James 2:1)

TJJohnson, (puzzle created 10.10.10)

Word, (John 1:1)

Names Jesus Known By, Part III
Various, KJV

Find and circle the words or phrases listed on previous page. Words can go across and down, and in three diagonals from left to right, up or down; right to left. You may also find unscripted words in the grid.

```
F  L  T  X  F  L  Z  L  C  C  N  F  X  N  H  G  K  Y  S  N  D
I  H  H  S  O  N  O  F  M  A  N  F  M  M  F  L  Z  U  O  R  E
R  R  E  T  N  G  P  K  T  H  R  Y  T  V  R  H  S  R  O  C  Y
S  D  F  M  J  T  C  H  M  L  Z  P  M  R  I  E  A  L  A  D  D
T  R  I  J  R  K  E  L  D  Q  F  N  E  G  J  H  E  E  Y  R  C
F  O  R  K  F  D  B  O  H  T  J  K  H  N  S  H  P  L  O  H  L
R  O  S  W  O  N  C  R  T  M  J  P  T  F  T  F  J  L  R  M  P
U  T  T  O  O  M  X  D  Y  L  R  R  O  H  O  E  E  Q  A  F  T
I  O  R  M  Y  R  Q  J  X  I  F  E  P  E  E  H  R  R  D  H  V
T  F  L  N  B  Y  D  E  E  M  S  G  C  R  T  E  Y  M  E  M  K
O  D  N  A  F  C  H  S  C  O  T  N  P  F  O  S  N  L  D  L  K
F  A  K  V  M  G  T  U  R  H  I  N  O  W  B  P  A  D  T  X  C
T  V  G  B  X  B  T  S  G  R  T  L  C  A  R  S  H  M  I  G  R
H  I  L  R  T  K  M  R  P  T  E  M  B  K  T  B  V  E  F  N  T
E  D  N  Z  V  X  Q  K  J  G  X  Y  H  H  G  P  G  N  T  T  G
D  B  R  I  G  H  T  A  N  D  M  O  R  N  I  N  G  S  T  A  R
E  Z  R  Z  N  K  K  A  V  L  J  E  S  U  S  C  H  R  I  S  T
A  C  L  A  M  B  W  I  T  H  O  U  T  B  L  E  M  I  S  H  H
D  W  C  Z  K  W  W  R  J  L  L  T  J  J  O  H  N  S  O  N  J
Z  N  R  V  K  S  E  E  D  O  F  T  H  E  W  O  M  A  N  Q  F
R  R  G  T  V  G  T  H  E  B  E  G  I  N  N  I  N  G  L  F  T
```

Parable of the Good Samaritan, Luke 10:25-37, KJV

Clues Across:

2.   The man who showed _ _ _ _ _ was considered a neighbor.
7.   In those days, Samaritans and Jews were not good _ _ _ _ _ _.
9.   One should love the Lord with all one's _ _ _ _ _ _ _ _, and (to 11D).
12. A parable is a story with a well understood theme that also has a _ _ _ _ _ _ meaning.
13. How much of your heart is sufficient to love God?
15. The Samaritan saw the fallen man and _ _ _ _ _ _ _ to help him.
19. In verse 27, the lawyer basically recanted the _ _ _ _ _ commandment.
20. In response to a question in verse 26, Jesus asked, "What is _ _ _ _ _ _ in the law?"
23. The lawyer wanted to find something to hold _ _ _ _ _ _ _   Jesus.
24. The Samaritan paid the inn keeper two _ _ _ _ _ _.
25. One must love their _ _ _ _ _ _ _ _ as themselves.
29. A _ _ _ _ _ _ even came by where the victim lay hurt, but did not stop.
31. The lawyer was intent upon _ _ _ _ _ _ _ Jesus.
32. Another aspect of loving the Lord is with all your _ _ _ _.
35. A _ _ _ _ _ _ passed by on the opposite side of where the fallen man lay.
36. Jesus was often referred to as a _ _ _ _ _.
37. The scribes and Pharisees were the keepers of the _ _ _ _ _.
38. The priest passed by the fallen man by moving to the opposite side of the _ _ _ _ _ _.
40. To _ _ _ _ _ in verse 34, means to bandage.
41. This puzzle content created by tj _ _ _ _ _ _, (05.18.05).
44. The lawyer asked what he could do to obtain _ _ _ _ _ _ _ life.
45. A pence is a Greek _ _ _ _ _ _ _ _.
46. The lawyer in this story was considered to by an _ _ _ _ _ _.
47. Thou shall _ _ _ _ the Lord thy God.

Down:

1.   The thieves took the man's _ _ _ _ _ _.
3.   The wine was used to _ _ _ _ _ _ the wounds of the man who was beaten.
4.   A pence is worth $32 American _ _ _ _ _, as of 1985. [1]
5.   (From 27D), _ _ _ _ _ _ _ could a Levite risk touching anything unclean.
6.   The law of _ _ _ is His Word.
8.   Jesus described one's neighbor with a parable about a _ _ _ _ Samaritan.
9.   The _ _ _ _ _ _ acted as a true neighbor.
10. Jesus told the lawyer to _ _ and do likewise.
11. (From 9A) . . . love the Lord with all your _ _ _ _ _, and . . . (to 43D).
14. The _ _ _ _ _ _ _ _ _ in parables are likened to things of a heavenly nature.
16. The Samaritan treated the man by pouring _ _ _ and wine on his wounds.
17. The Levite and the priest _ _ _ _ _ _ _ _ the Samaritan man.
18. The lawyer could also be called a _ _ _ _ _ _ _.
21. The wounded man was taken to an _ _ _.
22. Jesus told the lawyer that if he did according to his answer he would _ _ _ _ _ _.

Down Clues Continued:

26. The innkeeper was promised _ _ _ _ funds if necessary.

27. If a priest came near, or touched a dead body, he would be _ _ _ _ _, (to 5D).

28. The lawyer asked Jesus another _ _ _ _ _ _.

30. How many people passed near the fallen man?

33. The victim in this story is described as a _ _ _ _ _ _ _ man.

34. A Samaritan's _ _ _ _ _ was not purely Jewish.

39. In this parable, a man had been robbed and left half _ _ _ _.

40. The Samaritan proved to be a _ _ _ _ _ _ person than the Levite and the priest.

42. The Samaritan took good _ _ _ _ of the man in need.

43. (From 11D), . . . love the Lord with all your _ _ _ _ _.

1, Wayne A. Brindle, et al., *The King James Study Bible*. (Nashville: Nelson, 1988) 2033

The Good Samaritan, Luke 10:25-37

Parable of Planting Seeds, Matthew 13:1-23, KJV

Across:

3. Thorns, too much sun, and stones will _ _ _ _ a seed's chance to grown.
7. Many _ _ _ _ _ _ followed Jesus to hear what he would say.
9. Seeing they see _ _ _.
10. Verse one says that Jesus went out of the _ _ _ _ _.
11. Jesus sat by the _ _ _ _ _ _ _, (2 words).
12. The fruit produced a hundredfold, thirty-fold, even _ _ _ _ _ fold.
17. The first word of this parable is _ _ _ _ _ _.
18. A parable is told in _ _ _ _ _ form to relate everyday things with heavenly parallels.
20. Some seeds were burnt by the _ _ _.
22. Parables told about _ _ _ _ _ _ truths that were not apparent to all.
23. The seed that was planted properly brought forth _ _ _ _ _.
26. Many prophets desired to _ _ _ _ _ the things which Jesus told his disciples.
27. Jesus spoke to the multitude in parables while he sat in a _ _ _ _.
29. He explained to the disciples the meaning of the parables.
31. Those who hear the Word and don't understand are susceptible to the _ _ _ _ _ _ one.
34. Seed sown among thorns is likened to one who hears the word, but lets the _ _ _ _ _ of the world choke away fruitfulness.
36. Some seeds didn't have enough _ _ _ _ _ to find root in.
37. The Greek translation of 'Word' is _ _ _ _ _.
39. The sower seed parable fell in _ _ _ _ possible places.
40. _ _ _ _ to see.
42. Forthwith in verse five is the same as _ _ _ _.

Down:

1. The disciples' eyes and ears were considered _ _ _ _ _ _ _.
2. The people stood by on the _ _ _ _ _ as they listened to Jesus speak.
4. The sun burned some seeds because they didn't have _ _ _ _ _.
5. Hear _ _ therefore.
6. Trials and tribulation can cause a young Christian to be _ _ _ _ _ _ _ _.
8. However, some seed did fall onto _ _ _ _ ground.
11. A sower is one who plants _ _ _ _, (plural).
13. Parables of this puzzle fulfill the prophecy of _ _ _ _ _ _.
14. Fowls devoured the seeds that fell by the _ _ _ _ _ _ _.
15. The _ _ _ _ of the kingdom is revealed in the parables.
16. Unfortunately, some seeds fell among _ _ _ _ _ _, (to 35 D).
19. It is said that one will _ _ _ _ what one sows.
21. God's word has not had time to _ _ _ _ in new Christians.
24. This puzzle content created by _ _ Johnson, (12.10.04)
25. A bird is considered a member of the _ _ _ _ family.
26. This parable is called a _ _ _ _ _ _ _ parable.
28. He who has ears to hear, let him _ _ _ _ _.

Down Clues Continued:

30. The wicked one is considered to be _ _ _ _ _.
32. Thorns will _ _ _ _ _ the life out of a growing plant.
33. Jesus said that people's ears were _ _ _ _ _.
35. (From 16D); some seed even fell upon _ _ _ _ _ places.
36. _ _ _ _ to hear, (plural).
38. Hearing, they _ _ _ _ not.
41. Another word for behold is lo, or _ _ _.

Parable of Planting Seeds, Matthew 13:1-23, KJV

(Note: Numbers read from left to right, whether clue is Across or Down. Number of spaces in clue does not indicate number of letters in answer.)

Parables of The Lost, Luke 15:1-32, KJV

Across:

3. The lost coin parable involves a _ _ _ _ _ _.
4. The _ _ _ makers murmured against Jesus.
5. The young sojourner _ _ _ _ to himself.
7. The candle in verse eight refers to a _ _ _ _ _ _.
8. A shepherd is one who watches _ _ _ _ _.
9. The parable term for wasteful is _ _ _ _ _ _.
11. When he realized his mistake, the son determined to ask his father to _ _ _ _ _ _ him.
14. A piece of silver is worth about $32 American _ _ _ _ _ _ _ in 1985 money.
15. The father put a _ _ _ _ on his son's finger.
20. When one who was lost is found, people _ _ _ _ _ _ _ _.
22. One son asked his father to give him his _ _ _ _ _ _ before the appropriate time.
24. The father said, "thy brother was lost, and is _ _ _ _ _.
27. "My sheep _ _ _ _ my voice . . . ," (John 10:27).
28. This term also refers to wasteful.
31. These parables are about those who were _ _ _ _ _ _.
32. Nowadays, a silver piece is often referred to as a _ _ _ _ _ _, or a piece of change.
33. Puzzle content created by tj _ _ _ _ _ _ _, 12.10.04.
35. In this parable, Jesus talked to the publicans and _ _ _ _ _ _.
37. The wandering son's father had _ _ _ _ _ _ who were eating better food than he.
39. The citizen in verse 15 is considered a _ _ _ _ _ _ _.
41. The father told his servants to bring out the best robe and _ _ _ _ _.
43. The son who left home was the _ _ _ _ _ _ _ son.
44. The representative number of the lost in these scriptures is _ _ _.
45. This father said his son was lost, and also _ _ _ _.
46. Jesus asked, "What _ _ _ of you, having a hundred sheep . . ."

Down:

1. The Pharisees and _ _ _ _ _ _ _ criticized Jesus.
2. In verse two, receiveth translates as _ _ _ _ _ _ _.
3. The prodigal son _ _ _ _ _ _ his possessions.
4. This word translates to livelihood.
6. The father explained to the older son, that _ _ _ he had was his.
10. It was said that Jesus _ _ _ with the publicans.
12. A _ _ _ _ _ piece of silver is called a Drachma.
13. Joyous people usually don't celebrate alone, they invite several _ _ _ _ _ _.
16. One who was lost is celebrated over ninety _ _ _ _ righteous people.
17. There is _ _ _ in heaven over one lost sinner who repents, (see 19D).
18. The older son was _ _ _ _ because of the attention given to his brother's homecoming.
19. There is joy in the presence of the angels of _ _ _ when one sinner repents.
21. The inpatient son went into a _ _ _ country.
23. A fat _ _ _ _ was killed for the celebration.
24. From verse 18: "_ _ _ _ _ _, I have sinned against heaven and before thee."

Down Clues Continued:

25. There was a _ _ _ _ _ _ in the land during this parable timeframe.
26. He intended to ask his father to _ _ _ _ him as a servant.
29. A publican collects _ _ _ _ _ _.
30. Analogous word for wasteful described in this parable is _ _ _ _ _ _.
34. _ _ _ _ _ _ also refers to wasteful.
35. This chapter passage is often entitled 'the prodigal _ _ _'.
36. The hungry young man found a job feeding _ _ _ _ _.
37. The brother who left his home _ _ _ _ _ all that he had.
38. The father divided his livelihood between his _ _ _ sons.
40. Joy shall be in _ _ _ _ _ _ over one sinner who repents.
42. In each parable, 'lost' is a metaphor for a _ _ _ _ _ _.

Parables of The Lost, Luke 15:1-32, KJV

(Numbers read from left to right, line by line, whether clue is Across or Down.)

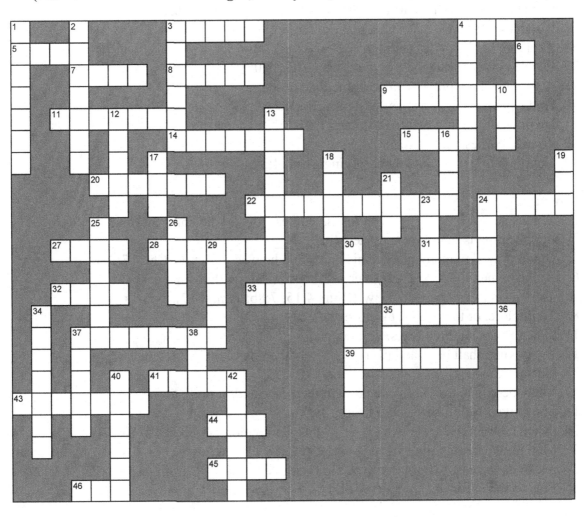

Pray A Prayer, No. 1, Various Scripture, KJV

Across:

1. The tax collector in Luke 18:13 _____ his chest.
5. God said He would be _____ to our unrighteousness, (Heb. 8:12).
6. Solomon and Daniel prayed with their faces turned toward _____, (1 Ki. 8:30; Dan. 6:10).
9. In prayer, one will often _____ upon God's goodness, (Phl. 4:8).
10. Thanksgiving is one day that most people remember to give _____ to God.
14. Matthew 6:6 tells us to go into our _____.
15. A prayer can be a request, _____, (Esther 5:7; Ps. 20:5).
16. When you pray, you are _____ God will answer you.
18. Solomon prayed with his hands stretched towards _____, (1 Ki. 8:22).
19. Jesus often prayed in _____, (Mark 1:35).
21. A prayer can be one of thanksgiving and _____, (1 Ch. 29:13; 23:30).
23. One person may intercede or _____ on behalf of another.
26. It is hard to accept a _____ answer to our prayers.
27. A prayer is a _____ made to God.
28. God already knows our needs, but He wants us to _____ anyway.
32. Christians pray to the Father in the name of _____, (John 15:16).
33. Notable cliché: A _____ and a prayer.
34. Ezra tore his _____, (Ezra 9:5).
37. Puzzle content designed by _____, (05.28.05).
38. A yes answer to prayer can be immediate or in the _____.
40. God's people _____ as they worshipped, (Neh. 9:3).
41. He prayed standing before the altar, (1 Ki. 8:22).
42. To urge earnestly.
43. Continue in _____ and thanksgiving, (Col. 4:2).

Down:

2. 'Let us have a little _____ with Jesus,' comes from an old spiritual song.
3. Supplication is said to be a request for _____.
4. David prayed in many places, this one while he was _____, (1 Chr. 17:16).
6. At the name of _____, every knee shall bow, (Phl. 2:10; Rom. 14:11).
7. To _____ is to violate God's law, (Rom. 4:15; 7:8b; Jam. 4:17).
8. To implore, or to _____, (Webster's).
11. God answers in three ways: yes, no, and _____.
12. Every knee shall bow, and every _____ shall confess to God, (Rom. 14:11).
13. Unrighteousness _____ the law.
17. Many people in the Bible prayed with their face and/or body to the _____.
18. She prayed within her heart, (1 Sam. 1:13).
20. When God forgives, He will _____ that sin no more, (Heb. 8:12, 10;17).
22. Men [& women] ought to _____ pray, (Lu. 18:1).
24. As far as the east is from the west, God removes our _____ from us, (pl) (Ps. 103:12).
25. Pray to the Father in _____, (to 36D).

Prayer, No. 1 Clues Down Continued:

29. Many people prefer to kneel on their _____ to pray.
30. To be forgiven of sin, one must _____ that sin to the Lord, (Rom. 10:9, Neh. 9:2-3).
31. Some people pray with their eyes _____ toward heaven, (Dan. 4:34; John 17:1).
35. Prayer can be in the form of a hymn, a chant, or a _____, among other things.
36. (From 25D) . . . and the Father will reward you _____.
39. _____ can be said to be no more than a silent prayer.

Pray A Prayer, No. 1,
Various Scripture, KJV

(Numbers read left to right, line by line, whether clue is Across or Down)

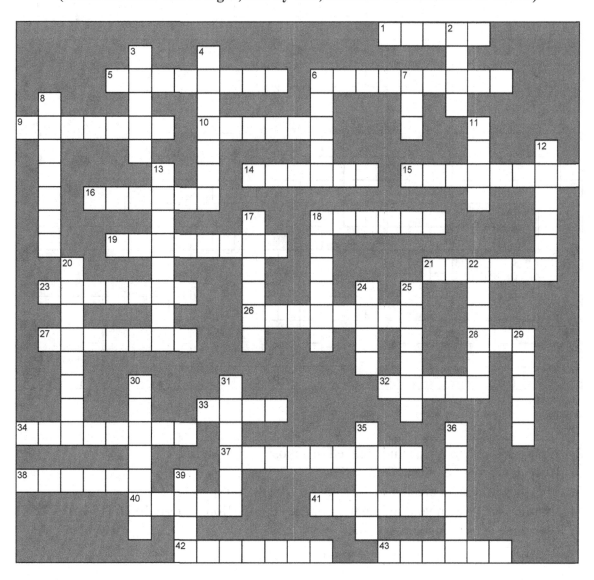

Pray A Prayer, No. 2
Various Scripture, KJV

(Note: Numbers read left to right, line by line, whether clue is Across or Down)

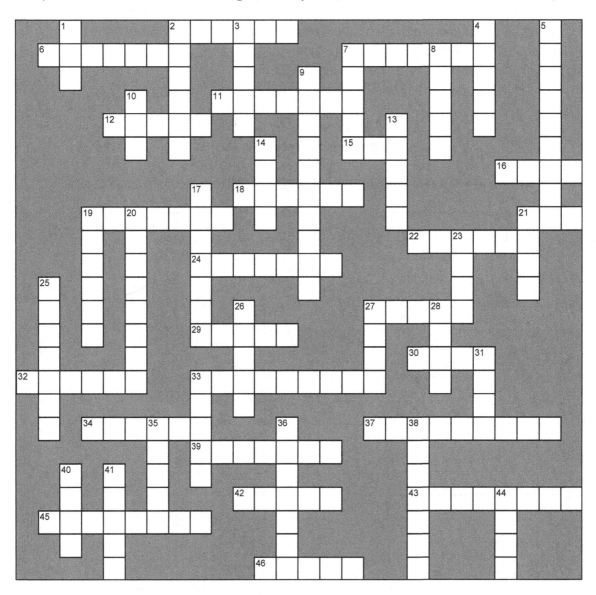

Across:

2. A prayer is reverent when it is prayed in a most _____ spirit.
6. If we don't forgive others, God will not _____ us.
7. This puzzle content created by tj _____, (05.28.2005).
11. 'If you _____ with your mouth the Lord Jesus . . .' (Rom. 10:9) (To 36 Down).
12. 'For thine is the Kingdom, and the _____ . . .'

Pray A Prayer, No 2 Clues Continued:
Across:

15. God gave his _____ to die in our place, (1 Cor. 15:3).
16. God will answer a believer's prayer according to His _____.
18. He sees in secret, but will _____ openly, (Mat. 6:6).
19. Some people pray to the God of _____, Isaac, and Jacob.
21. '____ and it shall be given . . .' (involves pre-requisites, Mat. 7:7).
22. It is wise to pray for _____, (James 1:5).
24. 'Thy _____ come, thy will be done; . . .' (Mat. 6:10)
27. Matthew 6:9-13 is said to be the _____ prayer.
29. I thank God for his _____ which provides forgiveness of our sins, (Eph. 2:5 & 8).
30. Bread can mean more than mere food, it also refers to the ____ of God, (see 27D), (John 6:35).
32. 'In all things, give _____,' (Eph. 5:20).
33. His grace covers a _____ of sins, (James 5:20).
34. When we pray we often say, 'Our _____,' (Mat. 6:9).
37. God hears a sinner's prayer if one is repenting to receive _____, (Rom. 10:11-14).
39. Everyone must _____ their sin to God to be forgiven, (1 John 1:9).
42. We must have _____ that God will answer prayer, (Gal. 3:22).
43. God will not forgive us if we don't forgive those who _____ against us.
45. If harmony is not in a marriage, prayer can be _____, (1 Peter 3:7).
46. Who said, ". . . men ought to always pray, and not lose heart," (Luke 18:1)?

Down:

1. Some prayers include these words: 'as humble as I know _____.'
2. 'On earth, as it is in _____, . . .' (Mat. 6:10).
3. Nothing but the _____ of Jesus can wash away our sins, (1 John 1:7; Rev. 1:5).
4. '_____, and the door shall be opened,' (Mat. 7:7).
5. Jesus taught his _____ a way to pray, in Matthew 6:9-13.
7. The Bible says to pray in the name of _____, (see Eph 5:20; Col 3:17).
8. (From 36 D), '. . . you shall be _____.' (Rom 10:9).
9. 'Lead us not into _____,' (Mat. 6:13).
10. Some people say, 'Father _____' when praying, (Ps 89:26; John 8:41; John 20:17).
13. (From 20D), Our Father _____ what we need before we even ask. (Mat. 6:8)

(Down clues continued, next page)

Pray A Prayer, No 2 Down Clues Continued:

14. '_____, and you shall find,' (Mat. 7:7).
17. When we pray we really are just _____ to God.
19. God wants to be _____, Rev 19:10; 22:9).
20. We must make known our _____ to God, even though, (Phil. 4:6) (to 13D).
21. 'Forever: _____,' (Mat. 6:13).
23. Jesus sacrificed himself on the cross to forgive the _____ of all the world, (Gal. 1:4; 1 John 2:2).
25. When we adore God, we _____ him.
26. 'Give us this day, our _____ bread,' (Mat. 6:11).
27. (From 30A), . . . which is also called the bread of _____, (John 6:35, & 48).
28. Jesus said 'I am the _____,' (John 10:7 & 10:9).
31. We don't have because we _____ ask, (James 4:2).
33. Not getting what we deserve is said to be God's _____.
35. God said to _____ your father and mother, (Mat 15:4).
36. (From 11A), '. . . and _____ in your hearts that God raised him [Jesus] from the dead . . . ,' (Rom. 10:9) (to 8D).
38. God will not honor a _____ request. (James 4:3).
40. Jesus commands that we do not use _____ repetitions when we pray, (Mat. 6:7).
41. Matthew 6 offers a _____ prayer.
44. Man [woman] should always _____, (Luke 18:1).

~ Your Thoughts on How You Pray ~

**Promise of Birth for Mary,
And Elizabeth*
Luke 1:1-38, KJV**

(Puzzle Grid on page 97)
*(Spelling: Elizabeth used instead of the Scripture's Elisabeth)
Across:

1. 'The house of' can be described as a _____.
3. With God _____ is impossible.
10. Course of Abijah can be translated as _____ of Abijah.
11. Luke claims to have had a _____ understanding of all things from the very first.
12. David was also described as the _____ of Jesus, (an ancestor).
13. Mary's son was to be named _____.
15. Nazareth is a city in the area of _____.
17. In verse 14, there is a promise of _____ and gladness.
18. Zechariah's son would be filled with the Holy _____.
20. To be espoused is to be _____, or engaged.
23. Both Zechariah and his wife were of the line of _____.
24. Mary was troubled at the angel's announcement because she was a _____.
26. The Holy Ghost would come upon John in his mother's _____.
27. The holy one born to Mary was called the Son of _____.
28. Zechariah's duty included the _____ of incense in the temple of the Lord.
30. The angel told Mary to _____ (2 wds).
33. Gabriel declared that he _____ in the presence of God.
34. Jesus will reign over the _____ of Jacob forever.
36. Before John was born, Zechariah and Elizabeth* did not have a _____.
39. This story occurred in the days when _____ was king.
41. Who wrote the book of Luke?
43. The angel who spoke to Mary?
44. While the incense burned, the people _____ outside the temple.
45. After Elizabeth* became pregnant she hid herself for _____ months.
46. Both Elizabeth* and her husband were quite _____.
47. Jesus will possess the _____ of David.

(Down Clues next page)

Promises of Birth Clues Continued:
Down:

2. The duty of burning incense in the temple was determined by drawing _____ .
4. He was sent by God to speak to Zechariah.
5. John was to drink neither _____ nor strong drink.
6. The angel told Zechariah to fear _____ , just as he had told Mary.
7. The power of the Most High was to _____ shadow Mary.
8. Mary was a _____ of Elizabeth.*
9. The angel told Zechariah that his _____ was heard.
10. Zechariah became _____ because he doubted the words of the angel of God.
11. Zechariah served as _____ in the course of his duty before God.
14. The name 'Jesus' means Yahweh is _____ .
16. The angel stood on the right side of the _____ .
17. Zechariah's wife would bear a son to be named _____ .
18. Many of Israel would turn to the Lord their _____ because of John.
19. Mary's baby was called the son of the _____ . (2 wds).
21. Joseph was of the house of _____ .
22. Zechariah would not speak again until after his son was _____ .
25. Under Jewish law, a betrothal was as binding as a _____ .
26. Zechariah and his _____ walked before the Lord blamelessly.
28. Both Zechariah and Elizabeth* were _____ righteous.
29. Mary said . . . , "be it unto me according to thy _____ ."
31. An _____ appeared to Zechariah while he was inside the temple.
32. The content of this puzzle designed by __ johnson, (12.10.04).
35. Elizabeth* was in her _____ month of pregnancy when Mary was visited by an angel.
37. Mary was described as being _____ favored.
38. Zechariah became _____ when he saw the angel.
40. John was a _____ of Jesus.
42. _____ had a vision where an angel urged him not to fret about making Mary his wife, (Matt 1:18-25).

*(Check spelling: Elizabeth used instead of Elisabeth)

Promise of Birth for Mary,
And Elizabeth,
Luke 1:1-38, KJV

(Note: Numbers read left to right, line by line, whether clue is Across or Down)

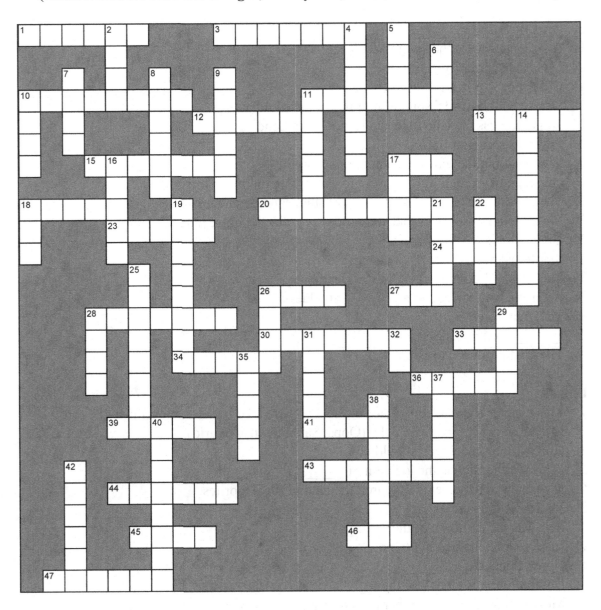

Remembering God's Promise
Deuteronomy 1:1-23, KJV

Across:

4. Burden or problem can be called a _____.
6. The law was written on stone ____.
7. _____ also spelled as Kedesh.
10. Area traversed in verse 19.
12. ____ gave Moses the law in Mt Horeb.
14. 'This side Jordan' refers to the ____.
16. Chiefs, or _____.
18. 'These be the words' sounds a lot like some of today's _____.
22. To go possess the land held suggestion of impending _____.
24. Sihon was king of the _____.
25. Who is doing the remembering in this story?
26. One man from each _____ went to survey the unknown territory.
28. The children of Israel had _____ over thousands, hundreds, fifties, etc.
29. Moses judged the cases that were too _____ for the other judges.
31. Israel, God's _____ people.
33. Seir translates as _____ or shaggy.
34. The land of Edom is _____ of the Dead Sea.
36. Astaroth, is described as a _____ goddess.
37. The great river.
38. _____ lived in Mt Seir.
39. The land promised to Israel.

Down:

1. This chapter's events took place in the _____ year of Israel's sojourning.
2. Mt Horeb is Mt Sinai; (Ex 3:1); (Oops, Sanai in answer grid).
3. God assured Israel they should not _____.
5. 'This side Jordan' is the location of _____.
6. ____ men were selected to search the land of the Amorites.
8. Mt Seir is the land of ____.
9. Seir was the patriarch of the _____.
11. Judges were charged not to be _____.
13. Horeb translates as _____.
15. Deuteronomy is a book of the _____.
17. Moses referred to the number of people as '_____' of heaven.
19. Kadesh-barnea translates as _____.
20. The captains suggested sending men to _____ the land before them.

Down Clues Continued:

21. The king of Og lived in _____.
23. _____ translates as star.
27. The Amorites were considered as Israel's _____.
30. The ground of Mt Horeb is said to be ____.
32. It is _____ days journey from Mt Horeb to Kadesh-barnea by way of Mt Seir.
35. Puzzle content designed by ___ johnson, 12.07.07.

Remembering God's Promise
Deuteronomy 1:1-23, KJV

(Note: Numbers read left to right, line by line, whether clue is Across or Down)

Samson,
Judges 13 - 16, KJV

Across:

3. God gives each of us a special _____.
5. Samson's father's name was _____
6. To make sport in this story means to _____.
10. The prize for solving Samson's riddle was _____ sheets & changes of clothes.
13. Samson ignored certain restrictions of his calling, but maintained his gift until he met _____.
15. The secret of Samson's strength was in his _____.
16. Israel learned to worship strange _____ because of their unlawful entanglements.
17. Before wrecking the building, Samson prayed, "Let me _____ with the Philistines.
19. Sheets as used in Samson's riddle are translated as _____.
20. The word jaw translates to _____ in Hebrew.
22. Samson asked God to strengthen him to avenge the loss of his _____ eyes.
23. The children of Israel were subject to the Philistines for _____ years.
26. Before his birth, Samson's mother had been _____.
27. Samson was destined to be a _____ from birth.
28. Samson's father-in-law was referred to as a _____.
32. In his anger, Samson carried a heavy gate up a _____ to Gaza.
33. Samson killed a lion and later ate _____ from the carcass
38. This puzzle composed by __ johnson, (09.24.05).
40. In a display of strength and anger, Samson tore away the Gaza city _____.
41. A Nazarite was not to touch anything _____.
42. Delilah shaved _____ locks of hair from Samson's head.
43. The wedding of Samson and his bride was celebrated for _____ days.

Down:

1. The angel of the _____ appeared to Samson's parents.
2. Because of his anger, Samson slew the hip and _____ of his wife's countrymen.
4. Samson destroyed the Philistines by pulling down _____ central pillars.
7. Israel continuously did _____ in God's sight.
8. Bound with fetters of _____, Samson was put in prison.
9. Delilah accused Samson of _____ about his strength.
10. Samson lied _____ times before telling Delilah the truth about his strength.
11. The woman Samson married was a _____.
12. The Philistines worshipped a god named _____.
14. The Philistines offered Delilah _____ hundred pieces of silver to betray Samson.
18. When Manoah realized who the angel was, he thought he and his _____ would die.
21. Before Samson was _____ he was destined to be special.
22. Samson judged Israel for _____ years.
24. A _____ in Gaza captivated Samson.
25. Because of Samson's being set apart, he was not to drink wine nor _____ drink.
28. Samson pulled down temple pillars killing about _____ thousand men and women.

Samson, Down Clues Continued:

29. The Timnite gave his daughter to Samson's best _____.

30. Samson _____ the restrictions of his Nazarite separation.

31. Delilah did not _____ Samson.

34. The Philistines put out Samson's _____.

35. To avenge his honor, Samson set fire to the tails of three hundred _____.

36. The woman Samson _____ was Delilah.

37. The wife of Manoah was warned not to eat anything from the _____.

39. During one battle, Samson slew 1000 men with the ____ bone of an ass.

41. Samson was a descendant of the tribe of _____.

Samson, Judges 13 - 16, KJV

(Note: Numbers read left to right, line by line, whether clue is Across or Down)

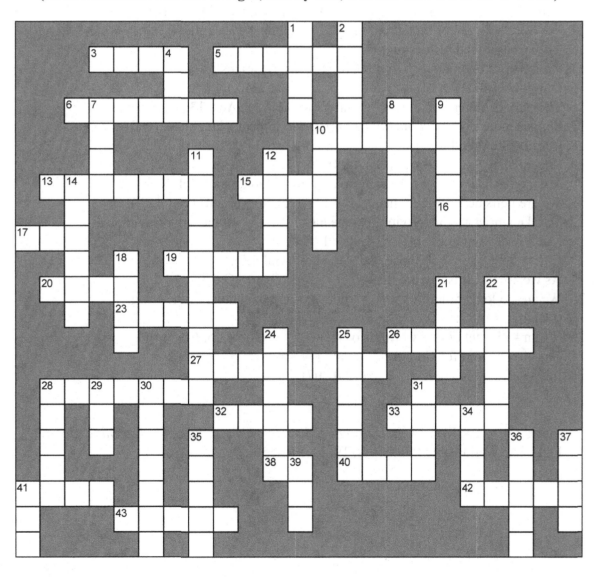

Sons and Daughters,
Various, KJV

Clues for Word Search on following page:

1. God _____ believers into his intimate family circle, (Romans (Rom) 8:15)
2. We live under the _____ of our heavenly Father, (2 Corinthians (Cor.) 10:8).
3. To receive Christ means you _____ in him, (Galatians (Gal) 3:22, 27).
4. 'Take eat; this is my _____ which is broken for you . . . ,' (1 Cor. 11:24).
5. Before Christ we were in _____ and spiritually immature, (Gal 5:1).
6. Sons as used here is generic for _____ or offspring, (Gal 3:28).
7. People covered by the blood of _____ are no longer in bondage to sin, (Rom 8:2, 10).
8. Sons and _____ are adopted, not just sons, (Gal 3:28).
9. We are children of God by _____, (Galatians 3:26).
10. God is our _____, (2 Corinthians 11:31).
11. 'And the word was made _____, and dwelt among us,' (John 1:14)
12. We were born not of blood, but of _____, (John 1:13, 1John 4:7; 5:1, 4).
13. The spirit of God resides in our _____, (Gal 4:6).
14. Christians are joint _____ with Christ Jesus, (Romans 8:17).
15. Our new birth is not of _____ origin . . . , (to #26), (John 3:5, 6).
16. The only begotten son of God, (John 1:18; 3:16, 18; Acts 13:33).
17. Son/s denote a _____ child but can refer also indicate daughters, (Gal 3:28).
18. Lord is often used to mean _____, (Matthew 6:24; 8:9; Mark 13:27; Gen 18:12).
19. We are all _____ in Christ, (Gal 3:28).
20. Jesus gave us _____ or the right to be sons of God, (John 1:12).
21. We are heirs according to the _____ of Abraham, (plural) (Gal 3:29).
22. To take Christ as your Savior also means to _____ him as your Savior,
    (Acts 2:38; Rom 5:17; Gal 3:14; Rev 17:14).
23. Christ came to _____ those under the law, (Gal 4:5).
24. As we are in Christ we are the _____ of Abraham, (Gal 3:7, 14).
25. We are no longer merely _____ but sons and daughters of the King,
    (Gal 4:7; Rev 17:14).
26. (From #15), but our new birth is of the _____, (John 3:5, 6).
27. The Greek word for God is _____, [1]
28. Initials of puzzle creator, _____; (12.07.07).

---

[1]   James Strong, S,T,D., LL.D., *Strong's Exhaustive Concordance Of The Bible*. (Iowa Falls, IA: World Bible Publishers, 1986), 544-550.

Sons and Daughters,
Various, KJV

Circle the answers that the clues on the previous page represent. Words can go across, down and in three diagonals. You may find unscripted words in the grid.

```
X  L  J  Z  H  S  H  N  D  N  K  F  P  G  M  W  X
T  J  L  U  U  M  G  Q  E  L  A  T  L  M  N  T  S
T  L  M  S  Q  M  M  R  K  T  C  H  R  I  S  T  E
N  A  E  R  K  N  D  G  H  N  T  Y  N  H  F  B  E
N  J  G  O  D  L  H  E  B  K  B  T  X  T  A  T  D
L  P  L  L  I  K  R  E  T  Q  M  E  H  B  I  N  S
W  N  J  H  R  T  T  K  A  Y  M  E  L  R  T  C  K
B  K  C  Q  M  A  L  E  B  R  O  A  Z  I  H  M  T
D  S  E  R  V  A  N  T  S  S  T  N  S  N  E  B  V
X  A  A  U  T  H  O  R  I  T  Y  S  E  T  O  V  R
R  C  U  K  R  M  D  M  O  T  G  S  P  N  E  T  E
T  E  D  G  R  W  S  M  N  Y  I  O  D  X  B  R  G
H  R  D  V  H  T  J  H  E  M  W  A  V  F  O  Q  N
E  W  F  E  P  T  S  N  O  E  G  G  M  F  D  M  X
I  R  Z  O  E  E  E  R  R  E  T  C  G  F  Y  T  L
R  X  D  J  L  M  P  R  R  E  C  E  I  V  E  M  D
S  A  N  F  D  F  J  H  S  R  K  S  P  I  R  I  T
```

The First Disciples
John 1:35-51, KJV

Across:

2. He whom Moses and the prophets wrote about.
5. Jesus said that there was no guile or _ _ _ _ _ in Nathanael.
7. Master is further translated as _ _ _ _ _.
9. Christ literally means the _ _ _ _ _ _ _ _ One.
12. Jesus was referred to as the _ _ _ of Joseph.
13. Peter translates as _ _ _ _ _.
15. John declared, 'Behold the _ _ _ _ of God.'
16. Two disciples of John the _ _ _ _ _ _ _ _ left him to follow Jesus.
18. This is the name Jesus called Peter, which means rock or small stone.
20. _ _ _ _ _, the son of God.
22. Matthew was one who collected _ _ _ _ _, (Mat 9:6)
24. God is the _ _ _ _ _ of Israel.
25. Jesus found Philip in _ _ _ _ _ _.
26. Jesus told Peter what his_ _ _ _ was when he first talked to him.
27. The tenth hour refers to _ _ _ _ o'clock a.m., (Roman time).
28. Messiah is interpreted as the _ _ _ _ _ _.
31. "Can any_ _ _ _ _ thing come out of Nazareth."
33. James and _ _ _ _ _ were both sons of Alphaeus, (Mk 2:14, Mat 10:3).
34. _ _ _ _ _ _ will open itself up and . . . (to 8D).
36. Peter had another name; _ _ _ _ _.
37. Andrew told his brother that he and others had found the _ _ _ _ _.
38. Jesus was of what city_ _ _ _ _?

Down:

1. Barnabas was a _ _ _ _ _ of Cyprus.
2. Andrew and his brother were sons of _ _ _ _ _.
3. Andrew had a brother named _ _ _ _ _.
4. The city where several of the disciples had grown up was _ _ _ _ _.
6. Verily translates as _ _ _ _ _ _, surely, or of a truth.
8. (From 34A) . . . , _ _ _ _ _ _ will ascend and descend upon the Son of Man.
10. Jesus referred to Nathanael as an _ _ _ _ _ _.
11. Jesus said to Philip, _ _ _ _ _ _ me.
14. The Greek word for verily is _ _ _ _.
17. One of the disciples who had followed John the Baptist was _ _ _ _ _.
19. Andrew, Peter, and _ _ _ _ _ _ grew up in the same city.
21. The first _ _ _ _ _ _ _ _ were personally selected by Jesus into his ministry.
23. Nathanael was _ _ _ _ _ about Jesus' abilities until Jesus talked to him.

First Disciples, Down Clues Continued:

26. Philip went to find _ _ _ _ _ to tell him about Jesus.
29. Author of this puzzle, 12.02.04.
30. Jesus said to the men following him, '_ _ _ _ and see.'
32. Rabbi in verse 38 is interpreted as _ _ _ _ _ _.
35. Jesus observed Nathanael under a _ _ _ _ tree.

The First Disciples,
John 1:35-51, KJV

(Note: Numbers read from left to right, whether clue is Across or Down; also number of spaces in a clue does not always match number of spaces in the answer.)

The Searchers, Deuteronomy 1:19-46
Exodus 18:13-27; Numbers 13-14, KJV

Across:

1. They were ordered to go back into the wilderness.
7. The people _____ they would be taken by the Amorites.
9. Some men reported back that the land was ____.
13. All except ____ people of that generation were refused entry into the new land.
14. ". . . I ____ not among you;"
15. Destined to lead Israel into the new land.
16. This puzzle created by _____, (12.07.07).
17. Unless God is with you, you will eventually be _____.
19. The Anakim were said to be_____. (pl.)
22. The people's hearts _____ because of their dismay.
23. Israel's _____ had no knowledge of good and evil.
25. An exception to the unbelieving scouts.
29. In another book the search party is referred to as _____.
31. Israel was encouraged to not be ____.
32. The searchers and the people _____ and would not go into the land.
34. The author of the books used for this puzzle.
36. To search out something secretly is to ____.
37. ____ by night.
40. The _____ land.
41. The searchers were comprised of _____ men.
42. Israel was pushed back into the land of _____ and destroyed.
44. God would not _____ to the voices of the people.
45. Israel was ready to do as the LORD required, but it was _____. (2 words)
46. To take an oath.
47. Wroth.
48. The people said the LORD _____ them.

Down:

2. Hearken.
3. God was angry with Moses because of Israel's _____.
4. The valley of Eshcol is located in ____.
5. Israel seemed to forget what God did for them in _____.
6. This story also retold in the book of _____.
7. The searchers returned with _____ of the land.
8. The land that Israel traveled for forty years was the wilderness of _____.
10. The people _____ God again and went to fight against the Amorites.
11. The advance team went up into a _____ before arriving at the valley of Eshcol.
12. Anakim translates as _____. (2 wds.)
13. "Yet in this _____ you did not believe the LORD your God,"
18. This man was also ready to take the land.
20. The Amorite people were greater and _____ than Israel.
21. ____ by day. (pl.)

Searchers Down Clues Continued:

24. This new land had abundant resources of milk and _____.

26. The _____ gave Moses the commandments to give to Israel.

27. The Amorite cities were _____ for protection against invasion.

28. Murmured.

30. Israel's children were chosen to _____ the promise land.

33. Prey. (pl.)

35. Presumptuously.

38. The assignment of the search party was to travel in this direction.

39. This skeptical, unbelieving generation were referred to as being _____.

40. Sware in v35. (past tense)

43. The land God gave to Israel was the land of _____.

The Searchers, Deuteronomy 1:19-46
Exodus 18: 13-27; Numbers 13, KJV

(Numbers read from left to right, line by line, whether clue is Across or Down)

The Widow, Unjust Judge, Pharisee, and Publican
Luke 18:1-17, KJV

(Numbers read from left to right, line by line, whether clue is Across or Down

108

Widow/Judge/Pharisee/Publican Clues:
Across:

1. Jesus said, 'Give to _ _ _ _ _ _ that which is Caesar's, (Mat 22:21).
4. Anyone who exalts himself will be _ _ _ _ _ _.
7. When the Pharisee prayed, he did so to _ _ _ _ _ _ (v11).
11. _ _ _, two, three . . .
12. The biblical term for an earthly story with a heavenly meaning.
13. Verse one speaks of _ _ _ _ _ in a parable.
14. The widow felt she had been unjustly _ _ _ _ _ _ _.
15. A conjunction that connects thoughts, ideas, sentences, etc.
17. Except you come as a little child, you shall in no _ _ _ _ enter into the kingdom of God.
18. Luke is said to have been a _ _ _ _ _ _.
20. A title often begins with _ _ _.
23. Jesus spoke of children as the _ _ _ _ _ _ of God.
26. The Pharisees were considered as _ _ _ _ people.
27. Jesus said, "_ _ _ _ _ _ them not."
28. A tax was collected in the _ _ _ _ _ _ Empire.
29. The publican simply prayed, "God be _ _ _ _ _ _ _ _ unto me, a sinner.
33. How many times a week did the Pharisee fast?
34. One man was justified, and one was _ _ _ _ _.
36. He told his _ _ _ _ _ _ not to rebuke people for bringing their children to him.
38. God's people _ _ _ to him day and night.
39. The publican _ _ _ _ his chest as he prayed.
43. Verse ten reads, 'Two men went _ _.'
44. The Pharisees thought themselves to be _ _ _ _ _.
45. There was a judge who _ _ _ _ _ _ not God.
46. Both the men _ _ _ _ _ as they were praying.
47. The widow asked the judge to _ _ _ _ _ _ her.
48. "When the Son of man cometh, shall he find _ _ _ _ _ _ . . . ?"
50. To exalt one's self is to _ _ _ _ yourself higher than you ought.
51. Even though he himself was unjust, the Pharisee thought others to be _ _ _ _ _ _.
55. A publican is one who collected _ _ _ _ _.
57. The story teller of the parables was _ _ _ _ _.
58. To suffer means to _ _ _ _ _, (v16) .
60. It is said that Luke wrote to explain the Gospel to the _ _ _ _ _.
63. The widow _ _ _ _ _ _ the judge and caused him to be uncomfortable.
64. In verse eleven, the Pharisee so much as named the publican as a _ _ _ _ _.
65. Jesus said, "_ _ _ _ _ _ little children to come unto me . . ."
66. Avenge is the same as _ _ _ _ _.

(Down Clues on next page)

Widow/Judge/Pharisee/Publican Clues:
Luke 18:1-17, KJV

Down:

2. The publican was _ _ _ _ _ _ _ to lift even his eyes to heaven.
3. God will avenge his own _ _ _ _ _ .
4. The publican stood _ _ _ _ off.
5. An infant is a _ _ _ _ .
6. The judge admitted that he didn't fear _ _ _, nor regard any man.
8. This is the same as 'verily.'
9. The two men in the story went to the _ _ _ _ _ to pray.
10. The Pharisees were said to _ _ _ _ _ _ _ certain other people.
12. Men ought to always _ _ _ _ .
16. The author of this book was a companion of Paul, and of _ _ _ _ _ .
19. The law makers _ _ _ _ _ to the law to make it fit their interpretations.
21. To be abased means to be _ _ _ _ _ .
22. The Pharisees had a puffed up _ _ _ _ _ .
24. Some people brought their _ _ _ _ _ _ _ to have Jesus touch.
25. The Son of _ _ _ refers to Jesus in this passage.
29. The Pharisee thanked God that he was not like other _ _ _ _ _ .
30. The widow and the judge lived in the same _ _ _ _ .
31. To _ _ _ _ , is to go without eating, or in some cases, drinking any liquids.
32. Jesus is _ _ _ _ .
35. The self-righteous man was proud that he paid his _ _ _ _ _ .
37. This parable was spoken unto the _ _ _ _ _ .
39. You could say that the widow _ _ _ _ _ _ the judge until he decided to help her.
40. The _ _ _ _ _ was described as unjust.
41. The Pharisee prayed about all the things _ _ had done.
42. Of the two men who prayed in (v10), one was a _ _ _ _ _ .
47. God identified himself as, "I _ _ " to Moses, (Exodus 3:14).
49. Luke is said to have also been a _ _ _ _ _ .
52. The Pharisees had contempt for anyone who was not a _ _ _ _ _ .
53. This puzzle content created by _ _ johnson, (06.30.05).
54. The publican was _ _ _ _ _ ; the Pharisee was not.
56. The publican's prayer was concern about his _ _ _ _ .
59. _ _ _ _ wrote the book of Luke.
61. A Pharisee is one who interpreted the _ _ _ _ _ .
62. Jesus is the _ _ _ of God.

What I Think I Know, For Sure,
Various Scripture, KJV

(Puzzle Grid on Page 113)

Across:

2. Another name for Bethlehem, (Gen 35:19).
5. John the Baptist was a _____ of Jesus.
7. Aaron and his sons were of the _____ office, (Ex 28, 29).
8. Puzzle content _____ by tjjohnson, (04.18.08).
10. The wise men _____ a star.
13. Jesus was called the _____ of God.
15. Used synonymously with Esau, (Gen 36:1).
16. 'Faith comes by _____,' (to 46A).
19. The price of Esau's inheritance was a serving of boiled _____, (Gen 25:31-34).
22. Jesus was born to a _____.
26. Father of Israel.
28. Mary washed the _____ of Jesus with her hair, (John 11:2).
29. (From 40A) . . . after he had been dead for _____ days, (John 11).
31. Twin brother of Esau.
34. A holy day.
35. He leads me in the path of _____.
37. _____ night.
40. Jesus brought him back from death, (to 29A).
41. The Baptist was Jesus' _____.
42. Esau sold his _____ to his brother. (could be hyphenated or 2 words)
45. 'The LORD is good; his _____ is everlasting', (to 20D).
46. (From 16A) . . . , 'and hearing by the _____ of God,' (Rom 10:17).
47. Moses' brother.
48. Jacob married two _____.
49. Blood on the doorframes of the Israelites meant that God would _____ them.

(Down Clues Continued Next Page)

What I Think I Know, Continued:
Down Clues:

1. Wife of Moses, (Ex 2:21-22).
3. He sought to kill baby Jesus, (to 21D)
4. Jesus healed the _____ and they walked.
6. (From 23D) . . . , 'I shall fear no _____.'
9. Bethlehem is called the city of _____, (1 Sam 20:6).
11. This tribe did not inherit land.
12. Jesus met a _____ at a well.
14. The father of Israel wrestled with an _____.
17. Adam gave names to all the _____, (Gen 2:19).
18. God brought _____ plagues upon Egypt when Pharaoh wouldn't let Israel go.
20. (From 45A) . . . , 'and his _____ endures forever.'
21. (From 3D) . . . So he commanded all boys under _____ years old to be killed.
23. '_____though I walk through the valley of death,' (to 6D).
24. Jesus described himself as a _____ vine, (John 15:1).
25. Samaritans were not considered as full-blooded _____.
27. Bethlehem is the _____ of Jesus, (Matt 2:1), (could be thought of as two words).
30. They were considered unclean.
32. O little town of _____.
33. John of the wilderness dined on _____, (Matt 3:4).
36. Faith is evidence of things not _____, (Heb 11:1)
38. There was no room in the _____, (Luke 2:7).
39. Moses fled _____ when he murdered a man.
41. John the Baptist wore clothes made of _____ hair, (Mark 1:6).
43. He who has an ear, let him _____.
44. Jacob fathered children of _____ women.

What I Think I Know,
For Sure,
Various Scripture, KJV

(Note: Numbers read from left to right, whether clue is Across or Down)

Words of Wisdom,
Various, KJV

Across:

1. Wisdom is with the _____, (Job 12:12).
6. God's _____ have wisdom, according to 2 Samuel 14:20.
8. He was the wisest king ever.
11. Joseph was wise in that he had reverence for, and _____ God.
12. 'Wisdom is a defense, and so is _____ . . . ,' (Ecclesiastes (Ecc.) 7:12) (to 21D).
14. Wisdom is a _____ in Deuteronomy (Deu.) 34:9, Exodus (Ex) 28:3, Is 11:2.
15. If we forget God's law, he promised to _____ our children.
18. Only the _____ gives wisdom and understanding . . .' (Proverbs (Prov.) 2:6).
23. Knowing how to do something is a _____ .
24. Knowledge describes _____ .
26. Luke 2:52, "Jesus increased in wisdom and stature, and in favour with God and _____ ."
27. The _____ of the righteous speaks wisdom, Psalm (Ps) 37:30).
29. This brings about contention, (Prov. 13:10).
30. 'Wisdom strengthened the wise more than _____ mighty men . . . ,' (Ecc. 7:19).
31. 'Wisdom is better than _____ of war . . .' (Ecc. 9:18).
32. 'Wisdom is the principal _____ . . .' (Prov. 4:7).
35. 'I will destroy the wisdom of the _____ ,' (1Corinthians (Cor.) 1:19).
37. Wisdom is said to have this in Ezekiel (Eze. 28:17).
38. 'He that increases knowledge, increases _____ .' (Ecc. 1:18)
39. 'Wisdom excels above _____ ,' (Ecc. 2:13).

Down:

2. He was blessed with skill in all learning and wisdom, (Daniel (Dan) 1:17)
3. Matthew wrote that people were astonished at the wisdom of _____ .
4. Wisdom can be destroyed or _____ . . . , (Eze. 28:17).
5. Proverbs 16:16 says it is better to get wisdom than _____ .
7. One who _____ will not find wisdom, (Prov. 14:6).
9. Is light better than darkness?
10. 'Let not the wise _____ in his/her wisdom . . .' (Jeremiah (Jer.) 9:23).
12. He was learned in the wisdom of the Egyptians.
13. The _____ of the Lord is the beginning of wisdom, (Prov. 4:7)
15. A _____ will despise words of wisdom.
16. If we reject knowledge, God will _____ us.
17. According to Proverbs 4:7, fear means _____ or reverence.
18. 'My people are destroyed for _____ of knowledge . . .' (Hosea 4:6)
19. '. . . one _____ destroys much good.'
20. . . . and he stretched out the _____ by his power and discretion, (Isaiah 45:12; Jer. 10:12)
21. 'The excellent thing is that wisdom gives _____ to those that have it.'
22. 'A child left to his own ways brings _____ , . . .' (Prov. 29:15).
25. Another word for destroy.
28. '_____ is the man/woman that finds wisdom . . .' (Prov. 3:13)

Down Clues Continued:

31. God's _____ are past finding out.
32. This puzzle created by _____ Johnson, (03.27.06).
33. 'In much knowledge is much _____ . . .'
34. Proverbs 7:4 refers to wisdom as one's _____.
35. This priceless gem comes from God.
36. _____ created the world by his wisdom . . .

Words of Wisdom, Various, KJV
(Numbers read from left to right, whether clue is Across or Down)

~ YOUR THOUGHTS ~

Chapter & Verse

Puzzle Solutions

APPENDIX A

Acts of the Apostles, No. 1
Acts 1-9, KJV

Acts of the Apostles, No. 2
Acts 10, KJV

1 PATIO
2 MAN
3 CAESAREA
4 TANNER
5 BAPTIZED
6 VISION
7 ITALIAN
8 COMMON
9 NATION
10 JOHNSON
10 JESUS
11 CAPTAIN
12 WORD
13 FRIENDS
14 APOSTLES
15 MILITARY
16 BAPTISM
17 TRANCE
18 RESPECT
19 THREE
20 BEASTS
21 THIRD
22 HANGED
23 ROMAN
24 CORNELIUS
25 FELL
26 LUKE
27 SHALL
28 ONE
29 SIXTH
30 DREAM
31 REFUSED
32 FEARED
33 ALL
34 JEWS
35 DOUBT
36 QUICK
37 OLD
38 PAUL
39 ANOINTED
40 UNLAWFUL
41 SHEET
42 GENTILES
43 TONGUES
44 GHOST
45 UNCLEAN
46 SAM
47 PERSON
48 ACCEPTED
49 VOICE
49 VESSEL
50 NINTH
51 PETER
51 PRAISE
52 JESUS
53 SINS
54 DAY
55 SIMON
55 SPIRIT
56 EATEN
57 GIFT
58 TIMES
59 SEARCH
60 GOOD
61 NOON
62 ONCE
63 ROCK
64 DEVOUT
65 LORD
66 THRICE

A Covenant Study
Various Scripture, KJV

A Letter of Concern-1
1 Thessalonians 1 & 2

A Letter of Concern-2
1 Thessalonians 3, 4, 5

A-6

Books of the New Testament

2	T	H	E	S	S	A	L	O	N	I	A	N	S	W	B	Z	B	T	L	L
1	K	R	T	B	L	X	2	P	E	T	E	R	W	Z	X	Y	K	N	T	K
L	C	D	E	H	P	Q	M	E	P	H	E	S	I	A	N	S	D	N	T	C
R	B	O	T	V	1	T	H	E	S	S	A	L	O	N	I	A	N	S	Y	O
C	J	C	R	G	E	M	A	R	K	S	K	Y	Z	W	T	K	N	H	J	L
P	N	W	N	I	K	L	N	K	N	C	H	C	E	X	L	W	T	R	A	O
Z	X	R	B	S	N	R	A	A	1	T	M	H	L	R	G	U	K	T	M	S
Q	M	X	T	V	E	T	I	T	O	J	T	V	G	R	N	T	K	N	E	S
C	T	C	T	T	F	T	H	M	I	T	O	M	T	M	W	M	C	E	S	I
V	A	G	E	D	A	R	I	I	A	O	V	H	N	T	X	R	M	M	2	A
G	H	P	P	L	X	T	K	M	A	C	N	O	N	I	X	C	M	N	C	N
2	1	E	A	H	1	G	H	L	G	N	M	L	M	T	L	R	C	L	O	S
T	T	G	B	H	I	K	T	K	W	E	S	M	M	U	P	H	V	N	R	R
J	K	I	M	R	H	L	B	K	L	V	F	W	G	S	Q	X	N	L	I	L
J	T	W	M	N	E	M	I	I	N	L	R	O	M	A	N	S	T	Q	N	T
O	J	R	F	O	G	W	H	P	L	D	R	N	N	T	M	N	V	B	T	T
H	K	W	D	F	T	P	S	X	P	Y	J	M	T	P	K	N	2	T	H	H
N	L	J	P	D	N	H	T	R	L	I	N	C	Z	X	H	L	J	N	I	M
S	Y	O	R	R	P	P	Y	M	R	K	A	W	X	O	M	D	O	K	A	Z
O	F	H	K	B	T	X	C	P	L	K	C	N	J	T	K	N	H	V	N	F
N	K	N	C	J	U	D	E	J	F	B	B	3	S	V	Y	V	N	D	S	T

Books of the Old Testament

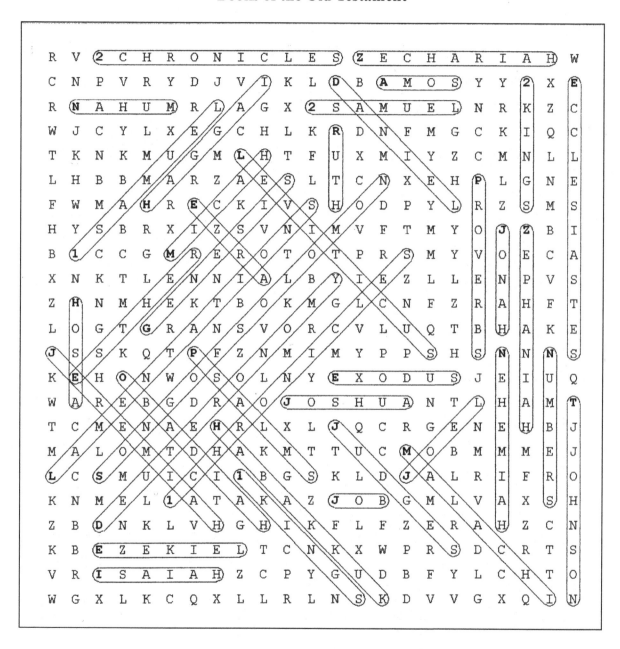

Faith And Temptation,
Jude

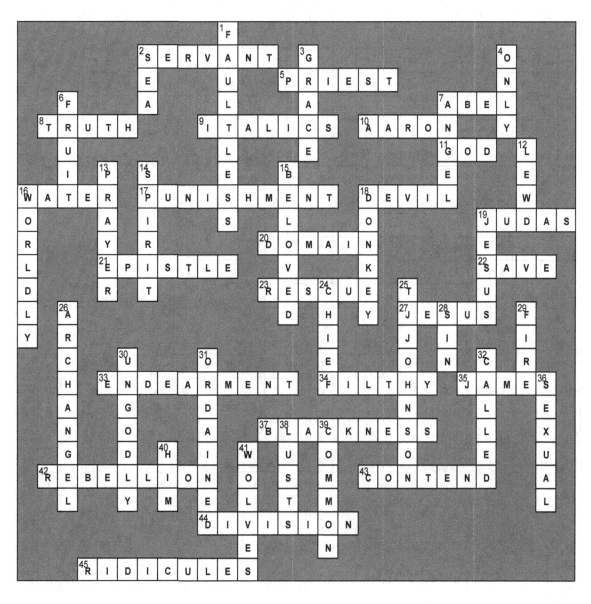

Gird Up Your Loins,
1 Peter 1:13-25

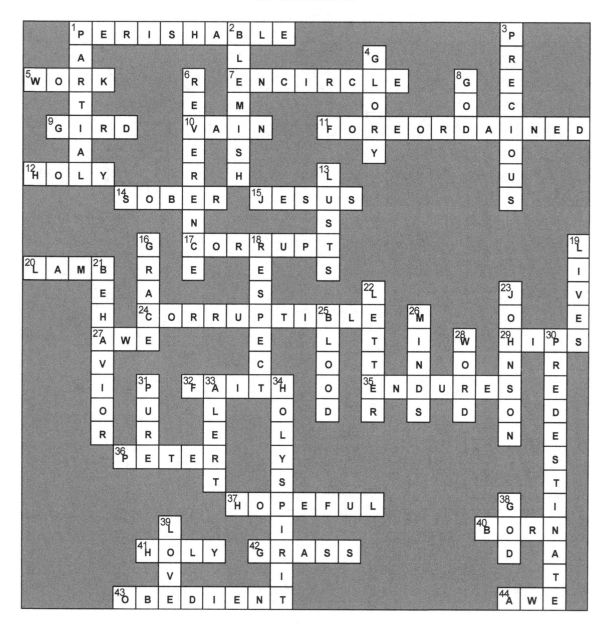

Go For What You Know
Various, KJV

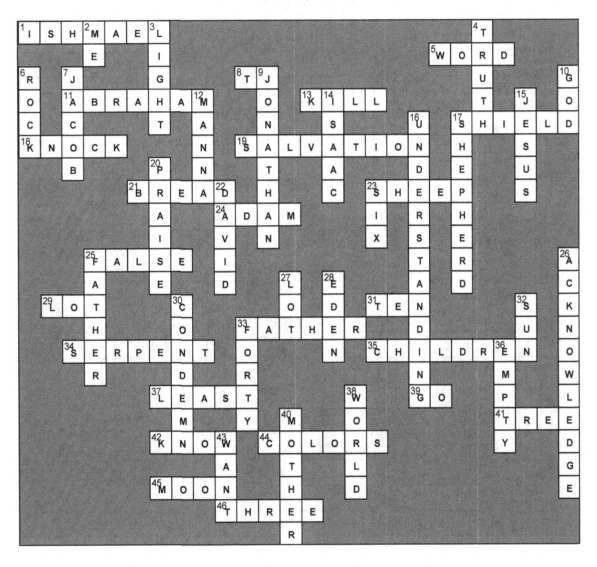

Goodness of the LORD
Various, KJV

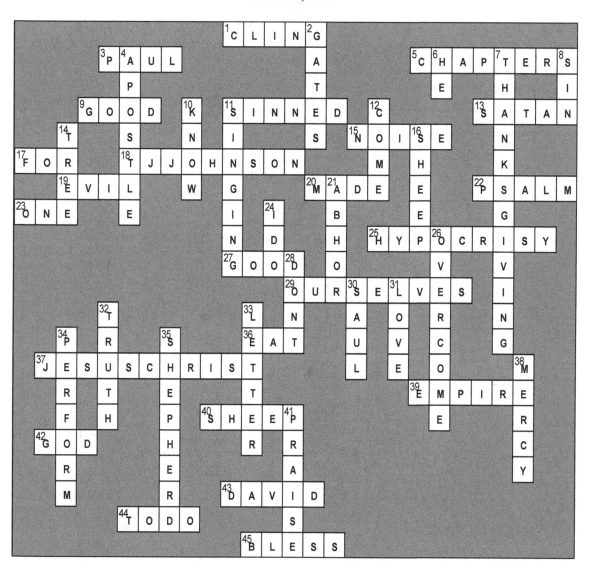

Grow In Christ
1 Peter 2:1-25, KJV

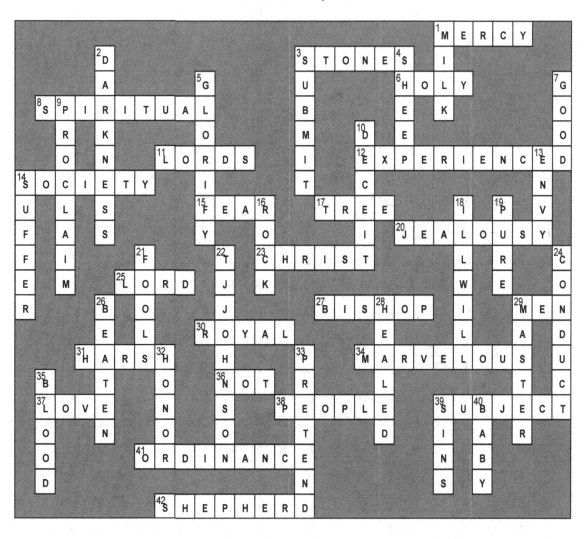

How Much Do I Really Know
Various Scripture

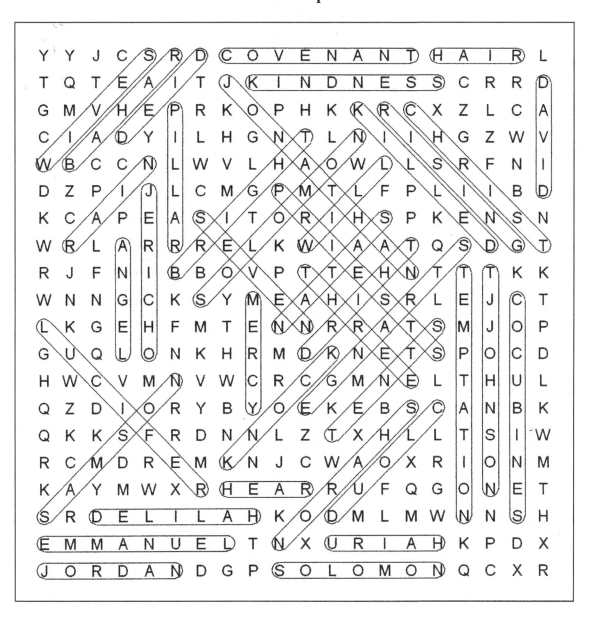

Israel's Only Redeemer, So Says Isaiah
Isaiah 1:1; 43:1-19

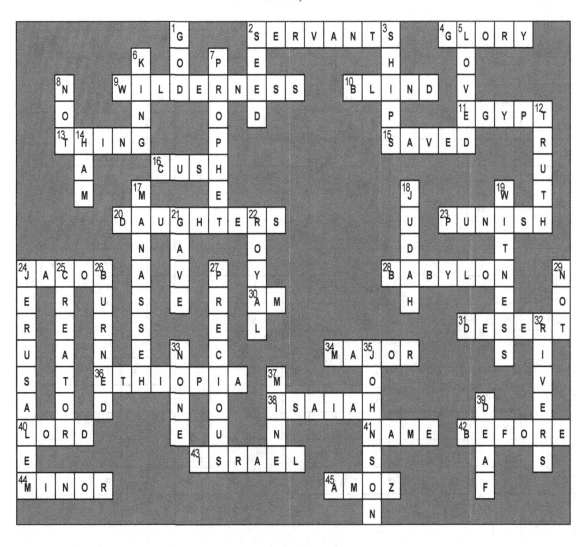

Jesus, According to John
John 1:1-34, KJV

1 BOSOM
2 JESUS
3 WORD
4 DWELL
5 MOSES
6 POWER
6 PREPARE
7 GOSPEL
8 WHO
9 SON
10 SAME
11 TRUE
12 JAMES
13 PETER
14 NAME
15 ELEVEN
16 BAPTIST
17 THUNDER
18 DINO
19 BEGOTTEN
20 TRUTH
21 FATHER
22 JOHN
23 DOVE
24 WITH
24 WITNESS
25 GRACE
25 GLORY
26 UNDERSTAND
27 TIME
28 MAN
29 RECEIVE
30 CHRIS
31 IN
32 RANKS
33 BORN
34 FALSE
35 FLESH
36 FISHERMAN
37 LOGOS
38 GLORIFIES
39 LIGHT
40 WORLD
41 LIFE
42 TJ
43 BEFORE
44 SONS
45 AFTER
46 ALL
46 AM
47 LOVED
48 HIM
49 GO
50 ONE
51 BELIEVED

Jesus And Nicodemus
John 3:1-21 (KJV)

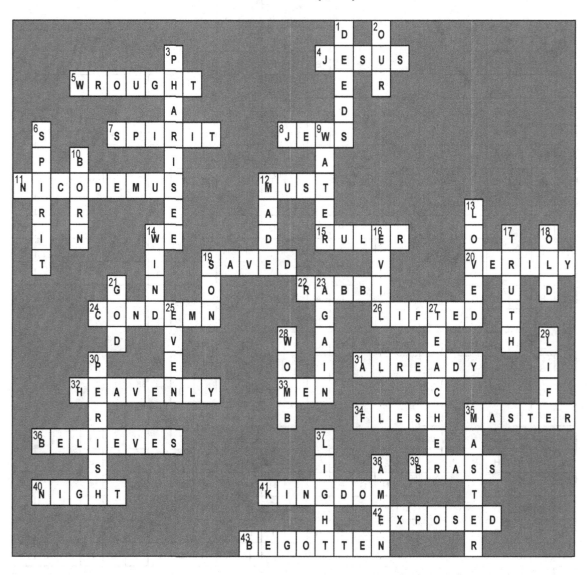

Jesus, Son of David
Matthew 1; 9:9-10, KJV

Jesus The Greater--John, The Lesser
Matthew 3

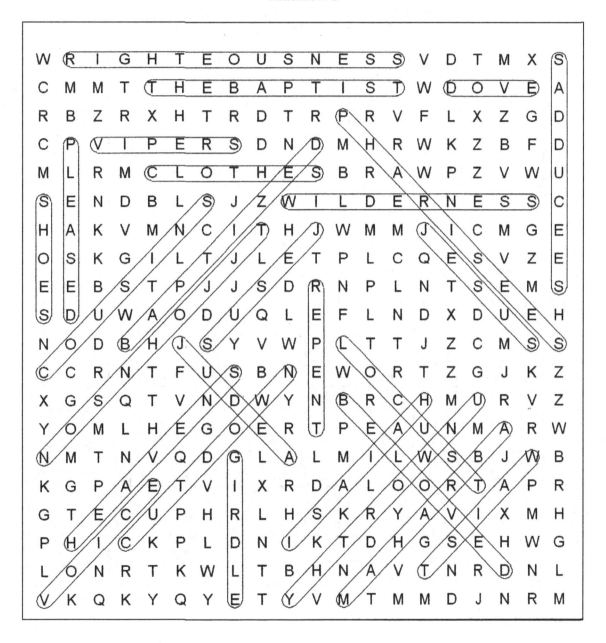

King Herod Plots to Kill the New King
Matthew 2, KJV

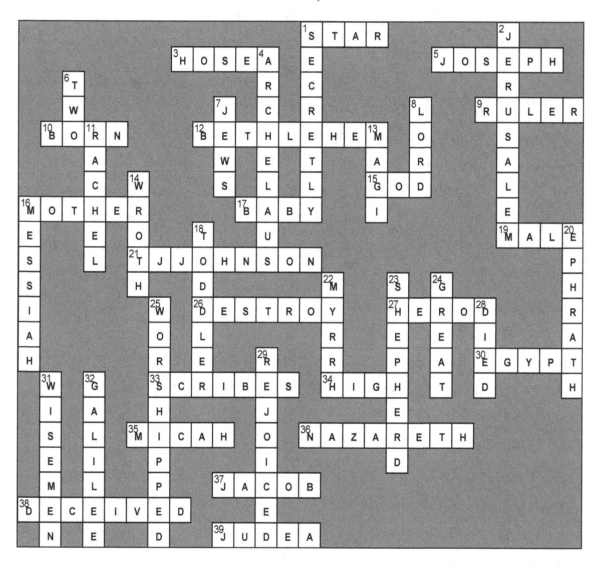

Letter To Galatians-1,
Galatians 1, KJV

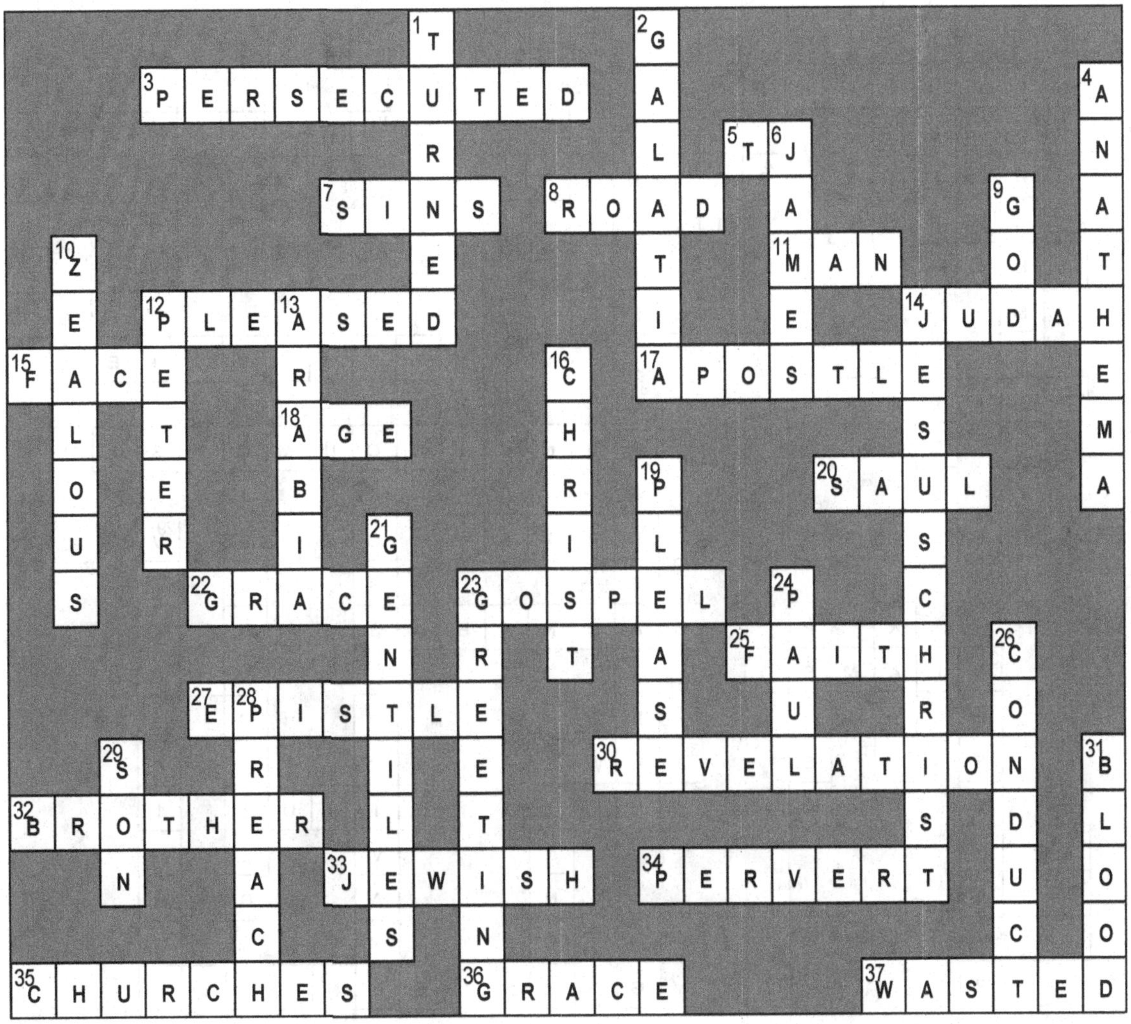

The crossword grid contains the following answers:

Across:
- 3. PERSECUTED
- 7. SINS
- 8. ROAD
- 11. MAN
- 12. PLEASED
- 14. JUDAH
- 15. FACE
- 17. APOSTLE
- 18. AGE
- 20. SAUL
- 22. GRACE
- 23. GOSPEL
- 25. FAITH
- 27. EPISTLE
- 30. REVELATION
- 32. BROTHER
- 33. JEWISH
- 34. PERVERT
- 35. CHURCHES
- 36. GRACE
- 37. WASTED

Down:
- 1. TREE
- 2. GALATIANS
- 4. ANATHEMA
- 5. T
- 6. J
- 9. GO
- 10. ZEALOUS
- 13. ABIDING
- 16. CHRIST
- 19. PLEASANT
- 21. G
- 24. PROCURED
- 26. COOL
- 28. PILATE
- 29. S
- 31. BLOOD

Letter To Galatians-2
Galatians 2, KJV

Letter To Galatians-3
Galatians 3, KJV

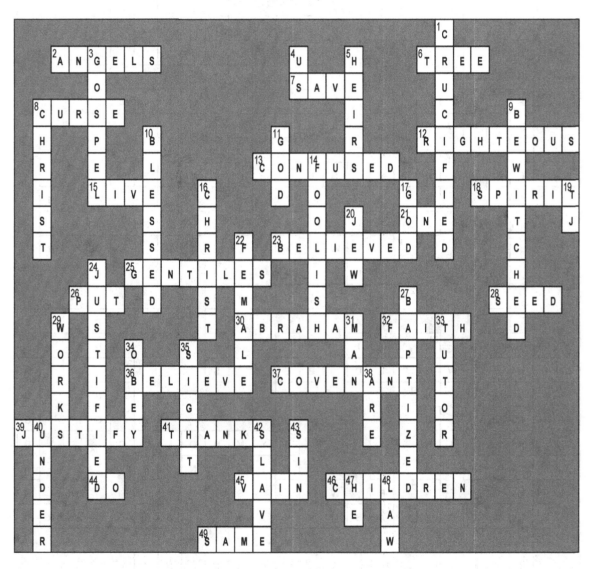

Letter To Galatians-4
Galatians 4, KJV

Letter To Galatians-5
Galatians 5, KJV

1 PAUL
2 LOVE
3 FREE
4 EFFECT
5 SUFFER
5 SPIRIT
6 EVIDENT
7 SELF
8 WHOLE
9 FRUIT
10 LIVE
11 INHERIT
12 FLESH
13 LEAVEN
14 DEBT
15 YE
16 LONG
17 BITE
18 ENVY
19 LIBERTY
20 RUN
21 NOT
22 THYSELF
23 GRACE
24 NO
25 OBEY
26 BEARER
27 HOPE
28 LIVE
29 YES
30 FAITH
31 ARE
32 LAW
33 CONCEIT
34 BY
35 CALLED
35 CRUCIFIED
36 DO
37 PEACE
38 CUT
39 UNDER
40 JEALOUSY
41 ADULTERY
42 HEED
43 HATRED
43 HAVE
44 JESUSCHRIST
45 TJ
46 WORKS
46 WALK
47 SON
48 ONE
49 FALSE
50 LED
51 YOKE

Letter To Galatians-6
Galatians 6, KJV

Luke's Genealogy of Jesus
Luke 3:23-38, 1:1-4, KJV

1 JOSEPH   3 AND   5 D   6 R   7 E
JOHNSON   2 P   8 P   O   E   E   X
9 SHELAH   10 PAUL   C
11 MARK   E   E
12 D   13 G   14 M   N   L
15 NARRATIVE   16 GRAND   L
17 M   E   18 W   E
19 L   20 THIRTY   21 NATHAN
22 JUDAH   I   T
23 B   24 SEVEN   C   25 C
26 GENEALOGY   28 THESON
27 E   29 J   30 NAMES   31 S
32 SHEM   33 PELEG   34 P   P
35 MOAB   36 TERAH
37 WAS   38 S   39 F
40 STORY   41 HELI
42 MARY
43 LAMECH
44 GOD
45 SON   46 ADAM
47 JESSE

A-27

Mary, Elizabeth, and Birth of John the Baptist
Luke 1:39-80, KJV

Moses
Exodus 1-4; Genesis 25,
KJV

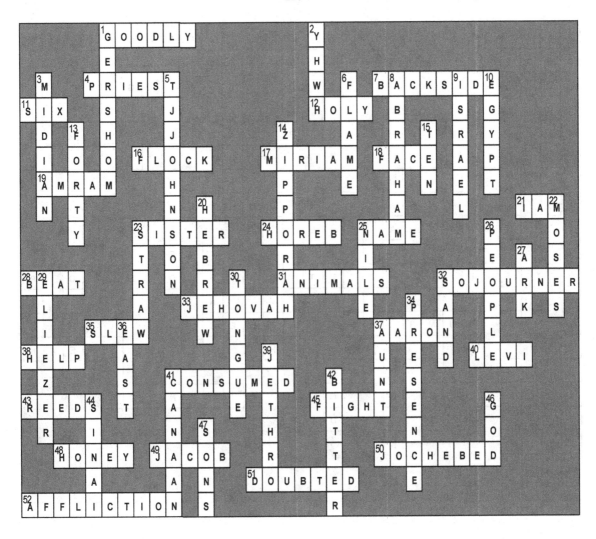

Moses Glimpses The Land
Numbers 20:2-13; Deuteronomy 3:24-29

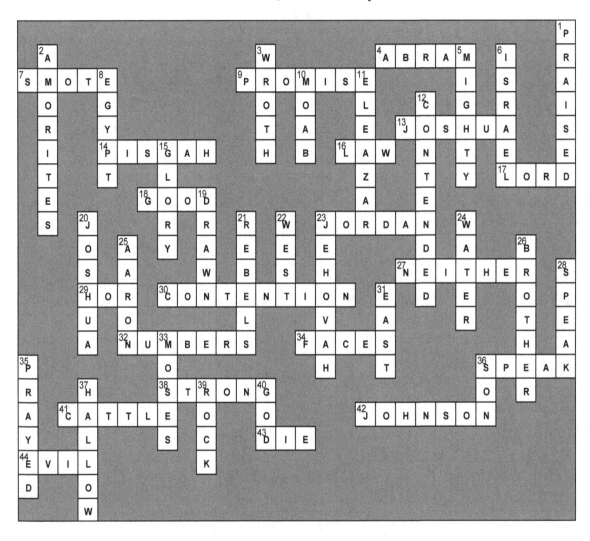

Names Jesus Known By, Part I
Various Scriptures, KJV

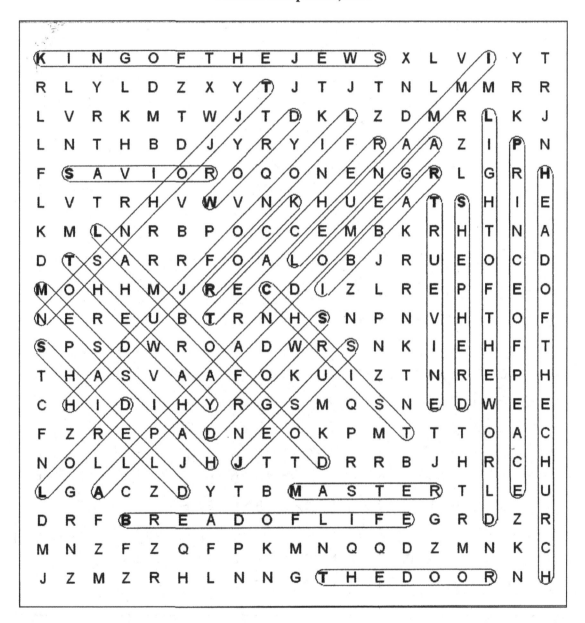

K I N G O F T H E J E W S X L V I Y T
R L Y L D Z X Y T J T J T N L M M R R
L V R K M T W J T D K L Z D M R L K J
L N T H B D J Y R I F R A A Z I P N
F S A V I O R O Q O N E N G R L G R H
L V T R H V W V N K H U E A T S H I E
K M L N R B P O C C E M B K R H T N A
D T S A R R F O A L O B J R U E O C D
M O H H M J R E C D I Z L R E P E O O
N E R E U B T R N H S N P N V H T O F
S P S D W R O A D W R S N K I E H F T
T H A S V A A F O K U I Z T N R E P H
C H I D I H Y R G S M Q S N E D W E E
F Z R E P A D N E O K P M T T T O A C
N O L L L J H J T T D R R B J H R C H
L G A C Z D Y T B M A S T E R T L E U
D R F B R E A D O F L I F E G R D Z R
M N Z F Z Q F P K M N Q Q D Z M N K C
J Z M Z R H L N N G T H E D O O R N H

A-31

Names Jesus Is Known By, Part II
Various, KJV

```
E V E R L A S T I N G F A T H E R J H L D K
W O N D E R F U L H P I M M A N U E L V M T
N F A I T H F U L W I T N E S S J F H J H T
H V B F N Z V M P K B R J C Z D M T Y O K H
Y T I P M Q Q K W Q X E A N O P U X L N B E
B H S R E N M P W L N G L G Z R L I Q D C F
T E H G S B N R C X E L Y O T N H W Z B Y I
Q W O T S N S V N M M T C E V S R H Z E B R
R A P B I K V O O X H N H J X E F R L T R S
F Y K G A L T D N G Q T F T B R D L P R I T
Q Y C M H J N G I O B R A N C H A S O L D B
T X L M Z A S M O B F P M D L V T L O H E O
G J Z R A G E O W O G D L R E W L Z K N G R
Z L J H M J N N N D J A H K E C J L J R N
R Q P O T R Z T Y O J S T V S L J B Z B O W
B L J H N R D Z F F F H N I T O N M N O M
A L D Z N C B W T O G U E K D H G C L M H
M R T K D Y S R R Y J O O D P L N E O M L P
G V K M G F Q O L L C W H D P H L R L S G P
J B C Y N F T I N P P N R W I T E X G I L Z
V G D K Z H L K M N D N R X A H N R L G F F
T S T E M O F J E S S E V B M M M L D C Y E
```

Names Jesus Known By, Part III
Various, KJV

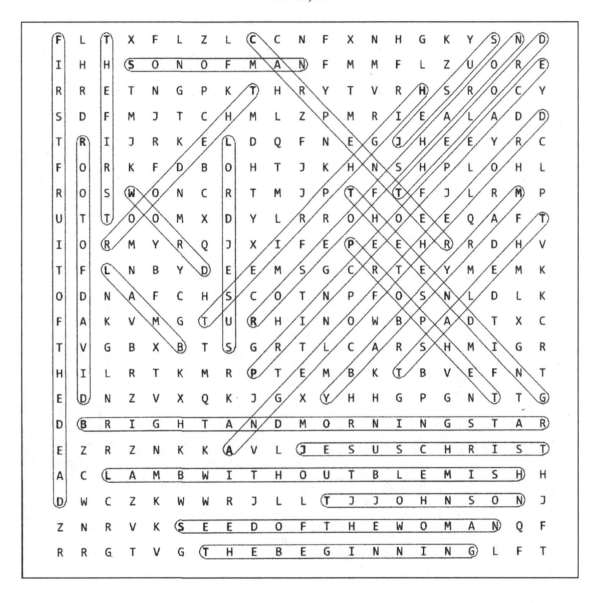

Parable of the Good Samaritan
Luke 10:25-37

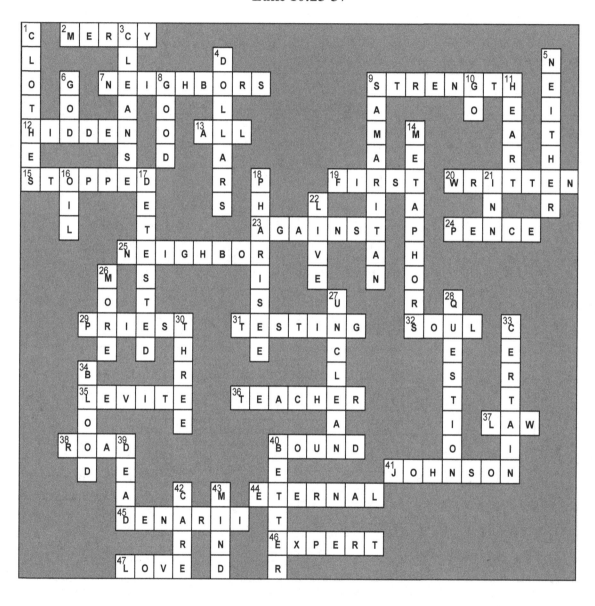

Parable of Planting Seeds
Matthew 13:1-23

```
                            ¹B
    ²S      ³K  I  L  L      L           ⁴R           ⁵Y                              ⁶O
     H         E              L      ⁷P  E  O  P  L  E                      ⁸G        F
     O         S                        O                                    O        F
     R         S              ⁹N  O  T                          ¹⁰H  O  U  S  E        E
¹¹S  E  A  S  I  D  E              ¹²S  ¹³I  X  T  Y                       D        N
  E            D                        S                                            D
  E         ¹⁴W                         A        ¹⁵W                    ¹⁶T            E
  D            A                        I           O                              D
¹⁸S  T  O  R  Y                         A           R        ¹⁹R        H
            ²⁰S  U  N        ²¹R     ²²H  I  D  D  E  N        ²³F  R  U  I  ²⁴T
²⁵F            I              O              A              N           J
  O            D        ²⁶K  N  O  W     ²⁷S  ²⁸H  I  P     ²⁹J  E  S  U  ³⁰S
³¹W  I  ³²C  K  E  ³³D     I     T           E                    A
  L      H            U     N           ³⁴C  A  R  E  ³⁵S     ³⁶E  A  R  T  H
      O            ³⁷L  O  G  O  S        R        T        A        A
      K            L           D        ³⁸H     ³⁹F  O  U  R        N
⁴⁰E  Y  E  S              O        ⁴¹S        E              N        S
            ⁴²I  M  M  E  D  I  A  T  E  L  Y
                        E                 R
```

Parables of The Lost
Luke 15:1-32, KJV

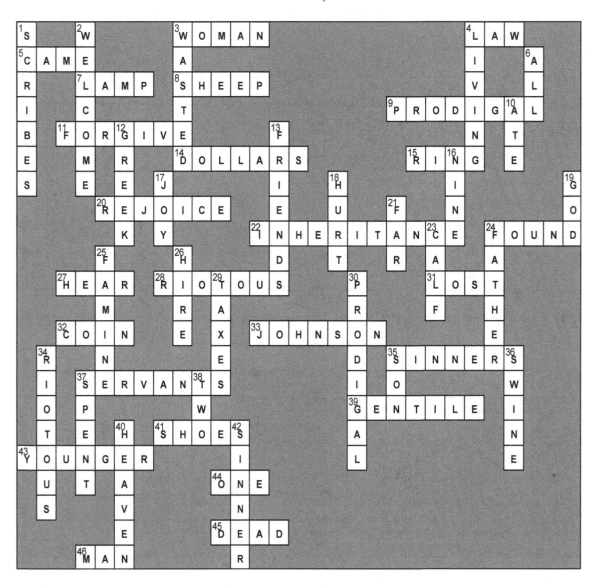

Pray A Prayer, No. 1
Various Scripture, KJV

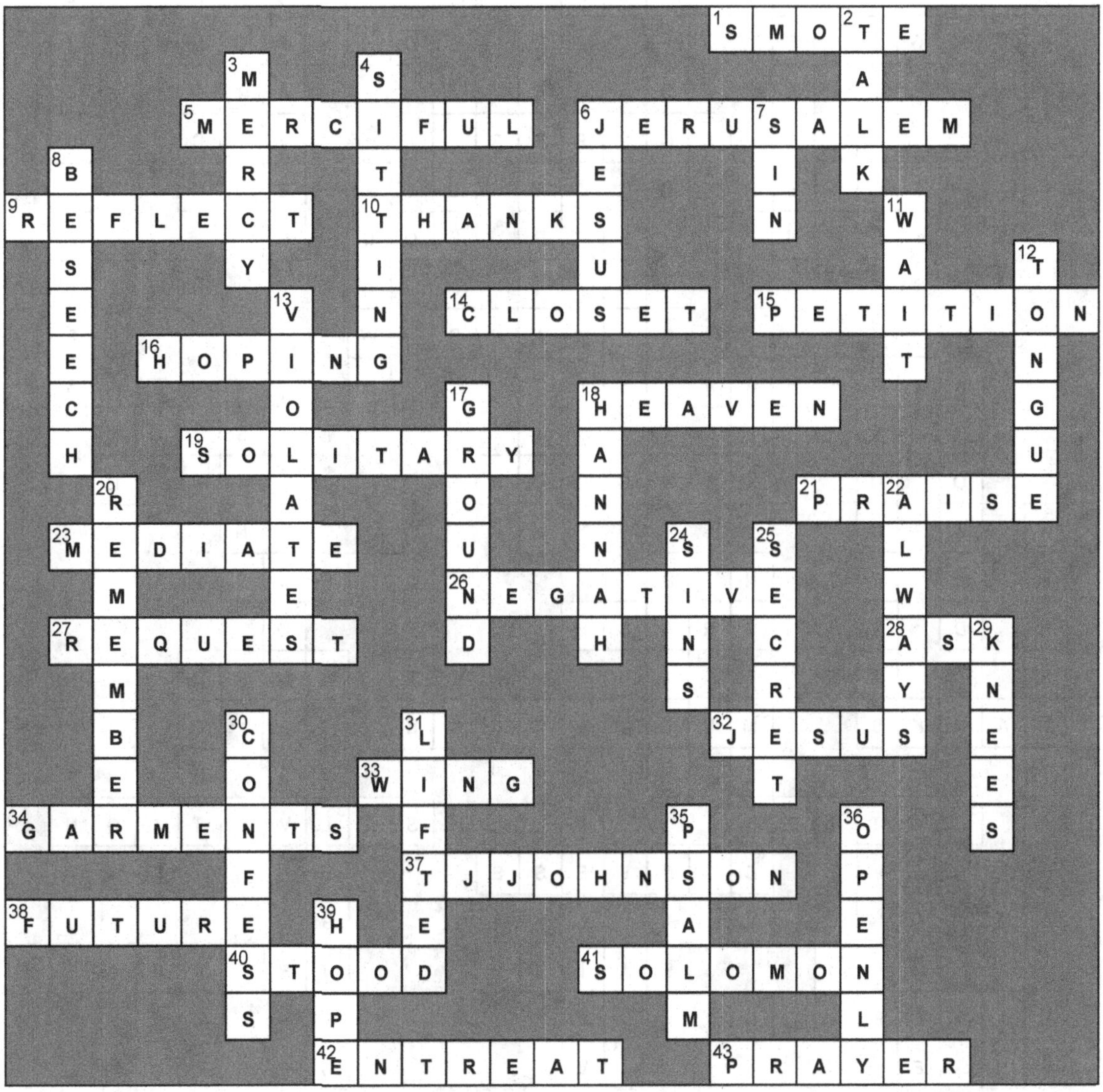

Pray A Prayer, No. 2
Various Scripture, KJV

Promises of Birth for Mary, and Elizabeth
Luke 1:1-38

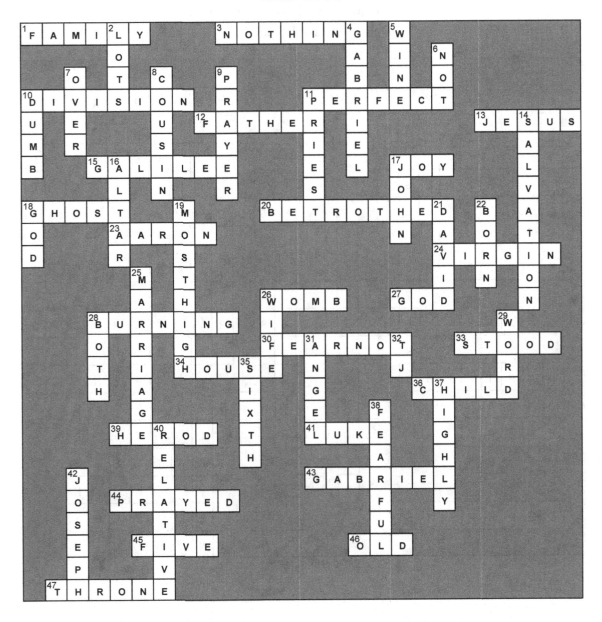

Remembering God's Promise
Deuteronomy 1:1-23, KJV

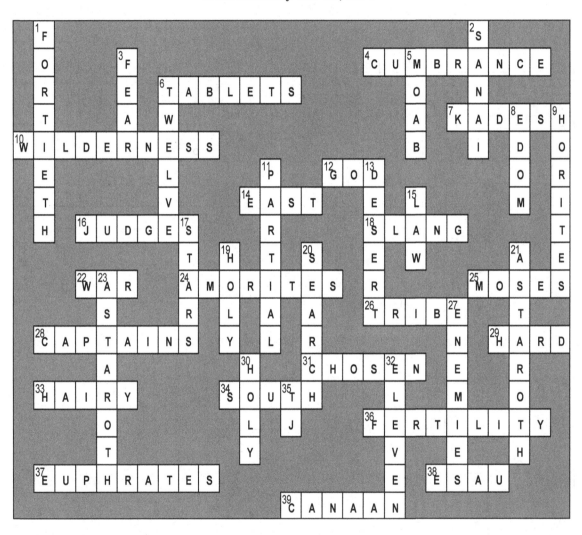

Samson
Judges 13 - 16, KJV

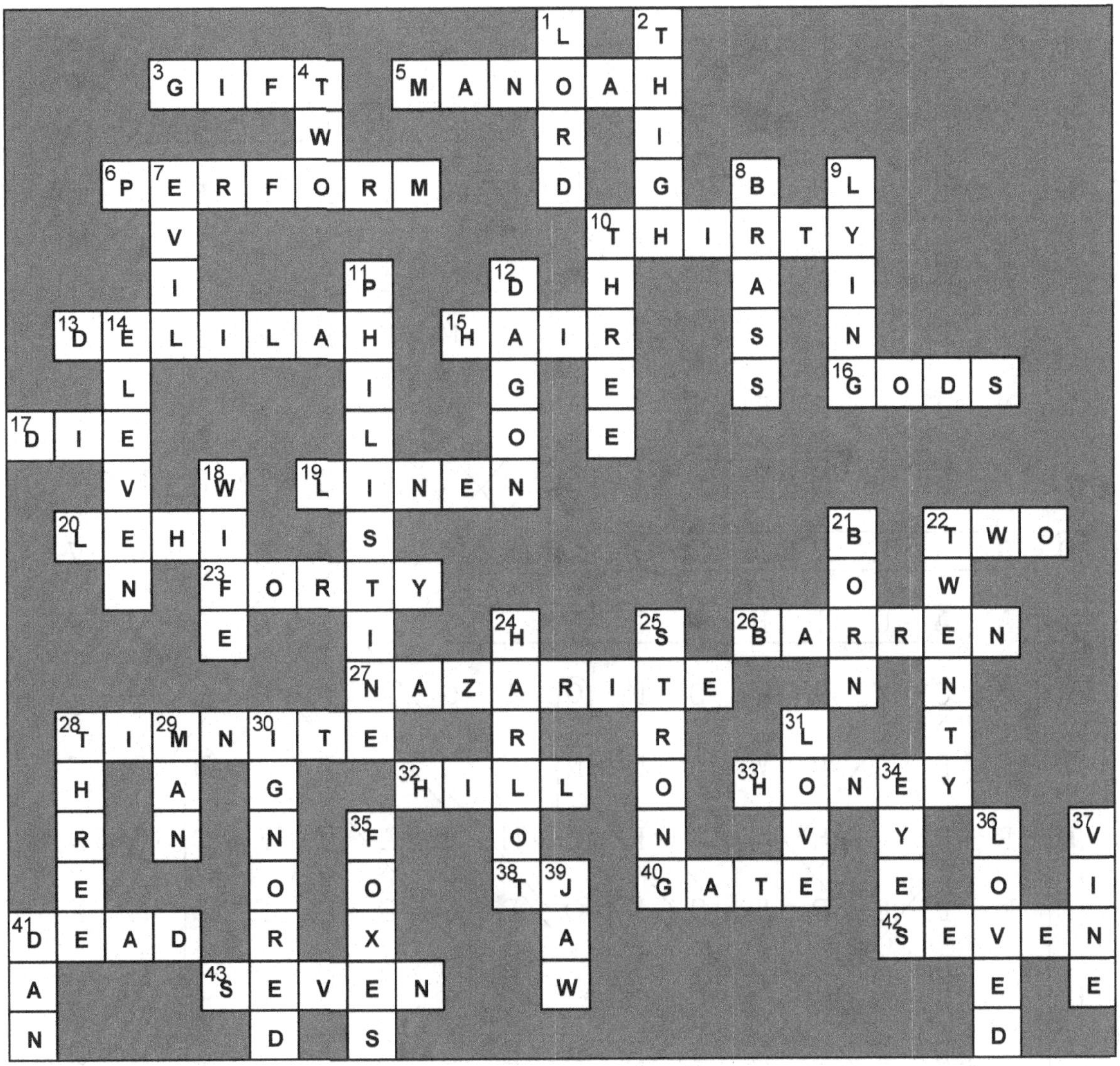

A crossword puzzle grid with the following filled answers:

Across and Down entries:
- 1 L
- 2 T
- 3 GIFT
- 4 TW
- 5 MANOAH
- 6 PERFORM
- 7 EVI (VI)
- 8 B
- 9 L
- 10 THIRTY
- 11 P
- 12 D
- 13 D
- 14 EL
- DELILAH
- 15 HAIR
- 16 GODS
- 17 DIE
- 18 W
- 19 LINEN
- 20 LEHI
- 21 B
- 22 TWO
- 23 FORTY
- 24 H
- 25 S
- 26 BARREN
- 27 NAZARITE
- 28 TIMNITE
- 29 MAN
- 30 ITE
- 31 L
- 32 HILL
- 33 HONEY
- 34 E
- 35 F
- 36 L
- 37 V
- 38 T
- 39 J
- 40 GATE
- 41 DEAD
- 42 SEVEN
- 43 SEVEN

Letters visible in grid:
L, T, GIFT, T, MANOAH, W, R, O, RI, G, PERFORM, V, D, G, B, L, I, THIRTY, P, D, H, A, Y, DELILAH, HAIR, S, I, G, R, N, DIE, I, E, E, GODS, V, W, LINEN, L, O, LEHI, I, B, TWO, N, FORTY, O, W, E, I, H, S, BARREN, N, N, NAZARITE, E, R, N, T, TIMNITE, MAN, ITE, R, R, L, T, HRE, AN, GN, HILL, HONEY, EY, R, N, O, V, Y, L, V, REE, FO, HOON, GATE, EO, I, DEAD, FOXS, TJ, SEVEN, ED, AN, SEVEN, DS, AW, N, ED, E

Sons and Daughters,
Various, KJV

X L J Z H S H N D N K F P G M W X
T J L U U M G Q E L A T L M N T S
T L M S Q M M R K T C H R I S T E
N A E R K N D G H N T Y N H F B E
N J G O D L H E B K B T X T A T D
L P L L I K R E T Q M E H B I N S
W N J H R T T K A Y M E L R T C K
B K C Q M A L E B R O A Z I H M T
D S E R V A N T S S T N S N E B V
X A A U T H O R I T Y S E T O V R
R C U K R M D M O T G S P N E T E
T E D G R W S M N Y I O D X B R G
H R D V H T J H E M W A V F O Q N
E W F E P T S N O E G G M F D M X
I R Z O E E R R E T C G F Y T L
R X D J L M P R R E C E I V E M D
S A N F D F J H S R K S P I R I T

The First Disciples
John 1:35-51, KJV

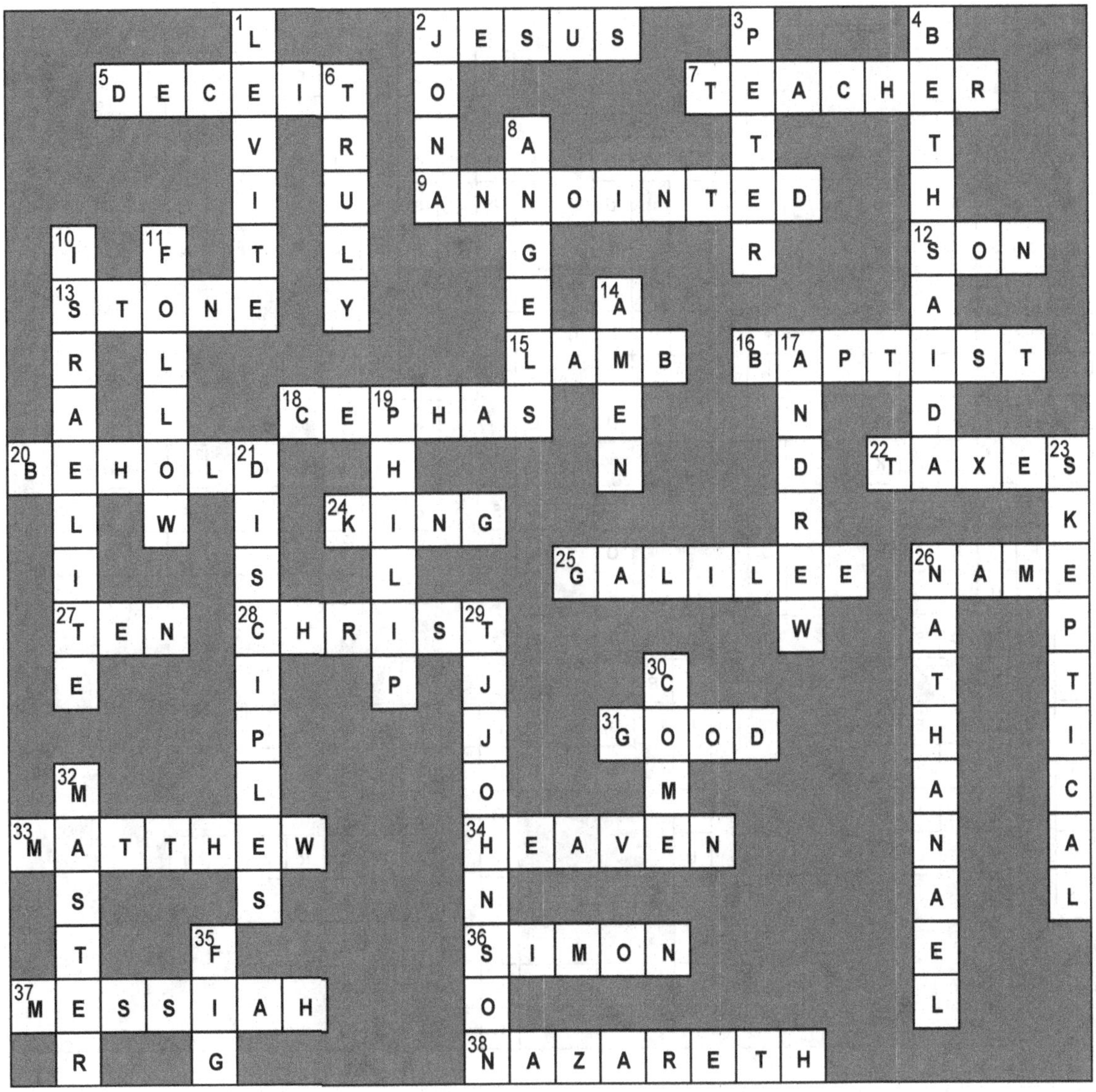

Crossword puzzle solution:

Across:
- 2. JESUS
- 5. DECEIT
- 7. TEACHER
- 9. ANNOINTED
- 12. SON
- 13. STONE
- 15. LAMB
- 16. BAPTIST
- 18. CEPHAS
- 20. BEHOLD
- 22. TAXES
- 24. KING
- 25. GALILEE
- 26. NAME
- 27. TEN
- 28. CHRIST
- 31. GOOD
- 33. MATTHEW
- 34. HEAVEN
- 36. SIMON
- 37. MESSIAH
- 38. NAZARETH

Down (letters visible in grid):
- 1. L
- 3. P
- 4. B
- 6. TRULY
- 8. A
- 10. ISRAEL
- 11. FILL
- 14. A
- 17. ANDREW
- 19. PHILIP
- 21. DISCIPLES
- 23. SKEPTICAL
- 29. TJJO
- 30. CM
- 32. M

A-43

The Searchers, Deuteronomy 1:19-46
Exodus 18: 13-27; Numbers 13, KJV

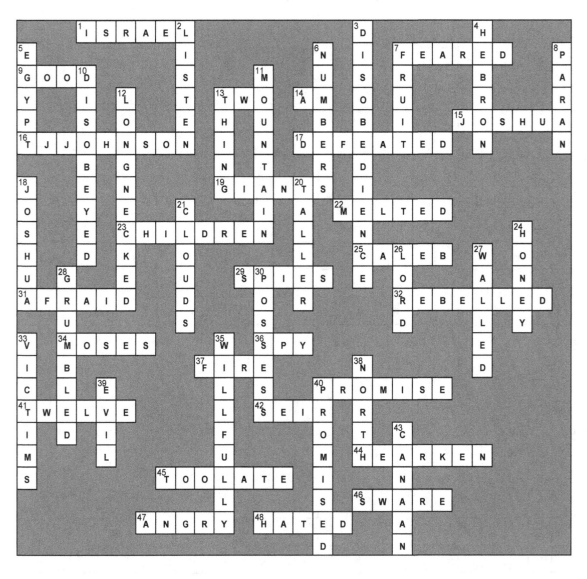

The Widow Unjust Judge-Pharisee-Publican
Luke 18:1-17, KJV

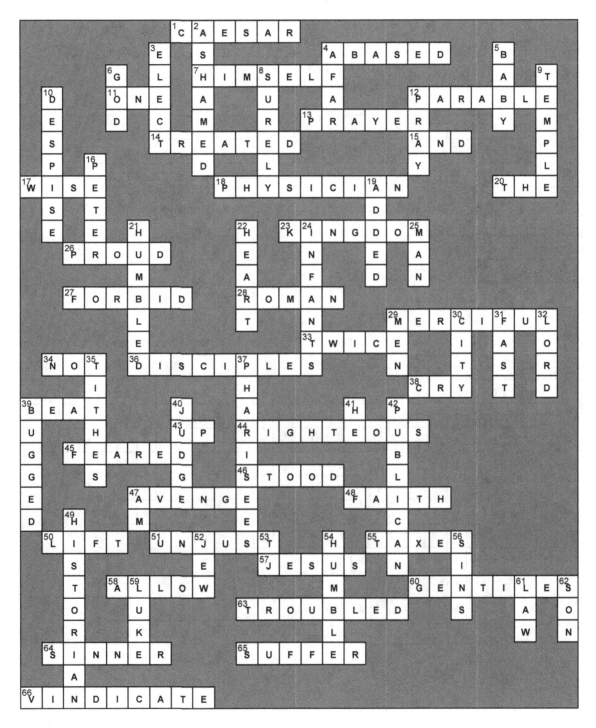

What I Think I Know, For Sure
Various Scripture, KJV

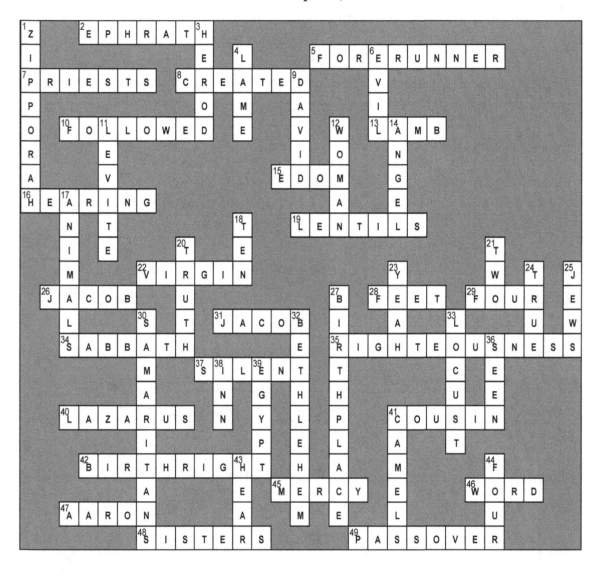

Words of Wisdom
Various, KJV

A crossword puzzle grid with the following filled-in answers:

Across
- 1. AGED
- 6. ANGELS
- 8. SOLOMON
- 11. OBEYED
- 12. MONEY
- 14. SPIRIT
- 15. FORGET
- 18. LORD
- 23. SKILL
- 24. PERCEPTION
- 26. MAN
- 27. MOUTH
- 29. PRIDE
- 30. TEN
- 31. WEAPONS
- 32. THING
- 35. WISE
- 37. BEAUTY
- 38. SORROW
- 39. FOLLY

Down (visible letter stacks)
- 2. D
- 3. J
- 4. CORRUPTED
- 5. G
- 7. SCORN
- 9. Y
- 10. GLORY
- 13. FEAR
- 16. R
- 17. R
- 19. S
- 20. H
- 21. L
- 22. S
- 25. P
- 28. H
- 33. GRIEF
- 34. S
- 36. G

Mostly Disciples
Various Scripture References

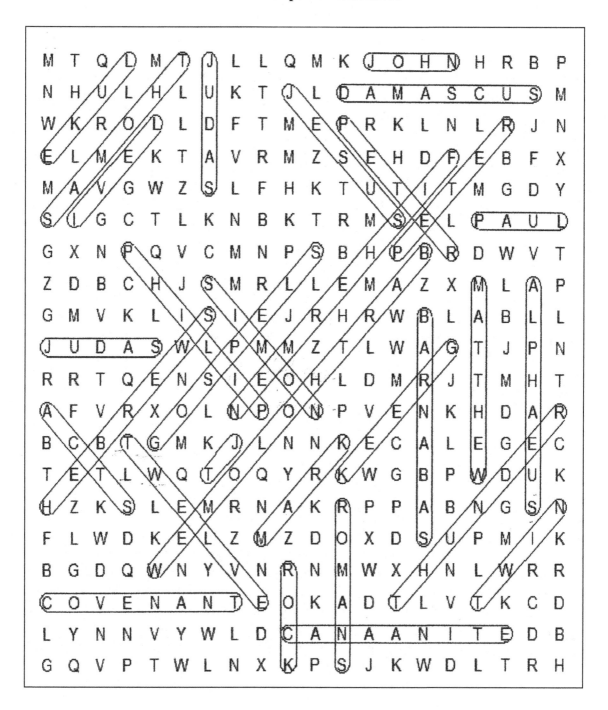

~ THE END ~

~ REFERENCES:

Bibliography:

Brindle, Wayne A., et al, eds. *The King James Study Bible*. Nashville: Nelson, 1988.

Bryant, Alton T., ed. *The New Compact Bible Dictionary*. Grand Rapids, MI: Zondervan, 1967.

http://www.blueletterbible.org

http://www.merriam-webster.com

Strong, James, S.T.D., LL.D. Strong's Exhaustive Concordance of the Bible. Reprint, Forty-Sixth Printing, Iowa Falls, IA: World Bible Publishers, Inc., 1986.

Unger, Merrill F., *Unger's Bible Dictionary*. Third Edition. Chicago: Moody, 1981.

Variety Games, Inc., Crossword Weaver™

A Word From The Author:

T.J. Johnson was lost and now is found.

For many years I searched to understand my life's purpose. I felt as if I just existed, not living life to its fullest. I earned a Bachelor's Degree in Information Systems from National University while I worked full time in the Computer Industry. Although this was satisfying it left me longing for something more. When I discovered my love for writing, and then teaching, I found the secret ingredient to my fulfillment.

I began journaling to help get myself through some very difficult times. In the early 1990s I went back to school for a semester of creative writing, but decided not to continue because of a loose sense of morality prompted by our 'freedom of speech' and thereby freedom of language in class and in writing assignments. I didn't feel comfortable in that environment so I enrolled in a home-study course with the Long Ridge Writers Group. This method of experimental writing served my purpose very well.

With my newly honed skills, I freelanced several years for *The San Diego Voice & Viewpoint*, my local neighborhood newspaper. Concurrently, I volunteered as writer and editor of my church's Newsletter. For eight years, I wrote Bible lessons for the National Baptist Convention of America, Inc. (NBCA, Inc.), which publishes quarterly Sunday School books that are distributed throughout the NBCA, Incorporated district of the United States. In 1999, my pastor recommended that I teach in our Christian Education department, so I began teaching Bible classes at my church, Bayview Baptist in San Diego, California. As of December, 2009, I am a contributing writer to our Studies in Christian Living curriculum.

I love Bible Study; I love teaching; and I love writing. My cup is not yet full, but I am full of joy! I know now what gives my life meaning and purpose! All Honor and Glory belong to God!

~ YOUR THOUGHTS ~

Other Books:

Chapter & Verse, Crosswords And Other Puzzles, Genesis Book One
Chapter & Verse, Crosswords And Other Puzzles, Genesis Book Two
The Genesis Men, Adam & Sons

Please address comments to guest notes on website: www.hayneskid.com